SECTS IN TIBETAN BUDDHISM

Emerging Perceptions in Buddhist Studies
(ISSN 0971-9512)

1-2. An Encyclopaedia of Buddhist Deities, Demigods, Godlings, Saints & Demons — with Special Focus on Iconographic Attributes; by Fredrick W. Bunce. 2 Vols. (ISBN 81-246-0020-1; set)

3. Buddhism in Karnataka; by R.C. Hiremath; with a foreword by H.H. the Dalai Lama (ISBN 81-246-0013-9)

4-5. Pāli Language and Literature: A Systematic Survey and Historical Study; by Kanai Lal Hazra. 2 Vols. (ISBN 81-246-0004-X; set)

6. Maṇḍala and Landscape; by A.W. Macdonald (ISBN 81-246-0060-0)

7. The Future Buddha Maitreya: An Iconological Study; by Inchang Kim (ISBN 81-246-0082-1)

8. Absence of the Buddha Image in Early Buddhist Art; by Kanoko Tanaka (ISBN 81-246-0090-2)

9. A Few Facts About Buddhism; by Gunnar Gällmo (ISBN 81-246-0099-6)

10. Buddhist Theory of Meaning and Literary Analysis; by Rajnish K. Mishra (ISBN 81-246-0118-6)

11. Buddhism as/in Performance; Analysis of Meditation and Theatrical Practice; by David E.R. George (ISBN 81-246-0123-2)

12. Buddhist Tantra and Buddhist Art; by T.N. Mishra (ISBN 81-246-0141-0)

13. Buddhist Art in India and Sri Lanka: 3rd Century BC to 6th Century AD — A Critical Study; by Virender Kumar Dabral (ISBN 81-246-0162-3)

14. The Tibetan Iconography of Buddhas, Bodhisattvas and Other Deities — A Unique Pantheon; by Lokesh Chandra & Fredrick W. Bunce (ISBN 81-246-0178-X)

15. The Dalai Lamas — The Institution and Its History by Ardy Verhaegen; (ISBN 81-246-0202-6)

16. The Tibetan Tāntric Vision; by Krishna Ghosh Della Santina (ISBN 81-246-0227-1)

17. The Buddhist Art of Kauśāmbī; by Aruna Tripathi: From 300 BC to AD 550 (ISBN 81-246-0226-3)

18. Mahāmudrā & Atiyoga; by Giuseppe Baroetto; Translated from Italian into English by Andrew Lukianowicz (ISBN 81-246-0322-7)

19. Theravāda Buddhist Devotionalism in Ceylon, Burma and Thailand; by V.V.S. Saibaba (ISBN 81-246-0327-8)

20. Faith and Devotion in Theravāda Buddhism; by V.V.S. Saibaba (ISBN 81-246-0329-4)

Emerging Perceptions in Buddhist Studies, no. 21

SECTS IN TIBETAN BUDDHISM

Comparison of Practices Between Gelugpa and Nyingmapa Sects

by

Vijay Kumar Singh

D.K. Printworld (P) Ltd.
New Delhi

Cataloging in Publication Data — DK
[Courtesy: D.K. Agencies (P) Ltd. <docinfo@dkagencies.com>

Singh, Vijay Kumar, 1963 –
Sects in Tibetan Buddhism : comparison of practices between Gelugpa and Nyingmapa sects / by Vijay Kumar Singh.
xv, 184 p. 23 cm.
(Emerging perceptions in Buddhist studies; no. 21)
Includes bibliographical references (p.)
Includes index.
ISBN 8124603308

1. Buddhist sects — China — Tibet. 2. Dge-lugs-pa (Sect) — China — Tibet — Customs and practices. 3. Rñiṅ-ma-pa (Sect) — China — Tibet — Customs and practices. I. Title. II. Emerging perceptions in Buddhist studies; no. 21.

DDC 294.39 21

ISBN-81-246-0330-8
First published in India 2006

Published and printed by:
D.K. Printworld (P) Ltd.
Regd. office : 'Sri Kunj', F-52, Bali Nagar
New Delhi - 110 015
Phones : (011) 2545-3975; 2546-6019; Fax : (011) 2546-5926
E-mail: dkprintworld@vsnl.net
Web : www.dkprintworld.com

Preface

RELIGION fascinates everyone. It becomes more evident in a country like India where it can be found in multiplicity. Barring one or two, the followers of every faith, religion or sect can be found in the Indian sub-continent. Every common Indian spends his/her life between the barriers of sin or virtue as per the established norms in his/her religious arena. But beside the diverse faiths, one common thread which always attracts me about religions prevalent in India that they all unequivocally advocate to living in harmony with every thing and each and every component of the universe. This hidden element of ecological balance is attracting more and more scholars towards itself than ever.

The study of Buddhism in general and Tibetan Buddhism in particular has always been an area which provides the researcher new heights of thoughts. Tibetan Buddhism is seen across the globe as the purest and unbroken form of Buddhism since more than thirteen centuries.

The prime role of Religions as I envisage is, at its minimum it harmonize the human beings and at its maximum it synchronizes the beings with the nature and the creator. It can be easily deduced that religion balances every being in its own position and try to maintain the equilibrium in the civilization with its components in its conceptual connotations. There were so many systems of the society that finally turned out to be a religion and so many religions that ultimately be called systems of life as they show a better way of life rather than preaching the rituals. Buddhism is one among the latter.

It is a well-known fact that Buddha never claimed to be an exponent of the religion. Instead, he said that I am giving you the way that can lead to salvation and help you out from the sufferings. So, we may term the Buddhism as a way of life rather than the dogma of rites and rituals. Therefore, it will be more appropriate to see the emergence of Buddhism in sixth century BC as a voice raised to purify the socio-ethical system of the then social order, to throw out the dogmatic views in order to establish the social and spiritual values in their illustrious manner rather than coming out as a new religious system. In fact, the emergence of Buddhism in that period was actually a revolt against the malpractices that were covering the true religious teaching of the Vedic culture. It was the need of time. Outside India also, we witness "Itsing"[1] in China and similar events of emergence of propagators of religious insurgency in whole world. In the light of above facts, we can see the Buddha as a reformer, one in the place of preacher of a new system or religion. Buddha tried to remove the darkness of the mind which he said is the basic cause of all suffering and that is ignorance.

But as we know, the forces of darkness are not outside but in the very inside of the human being who used to give thrust towards the triple coil of ignorance lust and hatred[2] that moulds the person to be self-centred and, here the base of defilements start playing its role. Therefore, though the highest teaching envisage the salvation in the end of any type of *karma*, good, bad or neutral; but for the common man, the teaching of Buddha starting with removing the ignorance[3] and then goes further up to higher planes with the last aim, i.e., enlightenment. My post-graduation with specialization

1. A Spiritual leader in China, the Jain *tīrthaṁkara* Mahāvīra was also dwelling in that period in India.

2. According to Buddhist theology, these three defilements are the root cause of every suffering of all the sentient beings. In Tibetan books they are considered as the prime debasements and every practitioner must remove himself/herself from these three emotions in order to purify and to go ahead in the Buddhist practices.

3. It is the root cause of our birth, sickness, old age and death.

in Tibetan studies, the living tradition of practising Buddhism since the time of Song Tsan Gampo, helped a lot to nurture interest in order to research deeply in the subject. My teacher in the post-Graduate classes, the Lama Guru Prof. Geshe Gelek Gyatso taught me Tibetan language and philosophy with his full compassion and wisdom for which the Tibetan Buddhism is famous worldwide. Therefore, first of all I seek his blessing and express my gratitude from the core of my heart. He not only provided me the valuable study material and photographs for my thesis but also pulled me out from the dilemma of mental blockade whenever I tucked myself during the course of writing. His Guru Kyabje Trijang Rinpoche's[4] blessing (the reincarnated lama who is in south India) was also very kind to me. I express my gratitude to him. I also express my sincere gratitude to my junior Tibetan teacher H.P. Gangnegi, Department of Buddhist Studies, University of Delhi who guided me on several occasions. Reverend Dr. Satyapal Bhikkhu, Reader in Pali also helped me a lot and gave me satisfactory answer to all of my queries regarding the Theravāda Buddhism.

Hence, the process of my second birth began (in the field of knowledge seekers; by the eradication of the ignorance).

Though Tibetan Buddhism is being studied all over the world at research level but very few research works are being done at home. Tibetan has lost their homeland and in India, the Sarvāstivādin school of thought was in vogue with the exception of the Himālayan region where the Mahāyāna is being practised since long. So many research works have been done by the scholars from United States and other countries, but most of them are limited to the translation works of the Tibetan Lamas visiting to States or elsewhere. Jeffery Hopkins, Alex Wayman, Michael Rosh is some of the names which have already gained popularity in this regard.

4. Kyabje Trijang Rinpoche, the junior teacher of the present Dalai Lama received the formal teaching from the Phabongkha Rinpoche, the illustrious exponent of the stages to the path.

Considering this, the research work on the ideologies of the schools of thought is not an easy one because there was not much of previous research work that could stand as precedent. But the intensity of the research work and the helping hand of my teachers encourage me to go ahead on the path of the research work assigned. I have undertaken this research work as a message for those who are practising the Buddha *dharma* in Tibetan tradition. This research work is a key to the intellectual practice of Buddhism in general and Tibetan Buddhism in particular.

I would like to thanks all the persons who have contributed and hence been instrumental to this piece of research work up to the completion. Thanks to my colleagues and friends who always remain the source of inspiration whenever I was morose and thought to give it up, they boosted my morale and suggested the ways to keep the study going on. Beside the fact that they were not connected to my subject, but always kept me pushing towards the goal. The names of Dr. Pankaj Malviya (Russian Dept.), Dr. Harjinder Singh (Chemistry Dept.), Dr. Vikas Bisht (Dept. of Mathematics), Dr. Virender Kumar (Sanskrit Dept.) all from this University and Dr. Md. Raziur Rahman (Dept. of Urdu, DDU University, Gorakhpur) are noteworthy. Dr. Mrs. Sudip Minhas (Lecturer in English Dept., PU, Chd.) helped me a lot whenever I sought. Prof. Aniruddh Joshi, Prof. Dhanraj Sharma and Prof. Shankarjiha of the Sanskrit department deserve more than thanks. They always guided and inspired me whenever I approached them with queries.

Swarn Singh, one of my friend and a computer expert helped me inserting the text into my PC tirelessly till the final print came out from it. I am thankful for his valuable assistance.

I want to thank all, who helped my work towards completion but due to the limit of space and my remembrance, I am constrained to mention all the names, but those names which have not appeared here, are as important as the names which have appeared here, I thank them also for their valuable contributions.

I thank my wife Seema who really worked as a hermit and did penances for creating a congenial atmosphere so that I may be able to come up with her expectation and complete this work. My two sons, both Atish and Asutosh kept me in jovial mood throughout the period and I here recall them for their love.

Last but not least I beg the blessings of my father Sh. Ramchandra Singh, a saint like person in his work who always insisted to go ahead in research and instructed me not to bother about the household affairs. The unlimited love and compassion of my mother Siyasundari Devi guided me thoroughly and keep me out of the troubles of life.

At the end, I would like to say that in the deepest feeling of my heart I can say that in reality, it was the compassion of almighty Buddha who guided me by these lines through the words of Nāgārjuna, who is considered as second Buddha:

नास्ति प्रज्ञा सम चक्षु नास्ति मोह सम तमम्।
नास्ति रोग सम शत्रुर्नास्ति मृत्यु सम भयम्॥[5]

The teachings of Lord Buddha are relevant immaterial of time. They were relevant in sixth century BC, today and will be relevant tomorrow. Buddha dreamed of world in which every sentient being live in harmony with each other.

5. *Prajñādaṇḍa*, verse 1.

Abbreviations

ADS	:	*Arya-Dharmasamgiti-Sutra.* Page-84b. Pechas gifted by Japanese govt. preserved in the DULS, Delhi
Auboyer	:	Auboyer, Jeannine, *Buddha, A Pictorial History of His Life and Legacy*
Bansal	:	Bansal, B.L., *Bon its interaction with Buddhism in Tibet,* Published by Eastern book Linkers, Delhi
Bhutia	:	Bhutia, Dr. T.D., *Beyond Eternity through Mysticism*
DIIR	:	Department of Information and International Relation, Central Tibetan Administration, Dharamsala, H.P., India
Dhamma	:	*The Dhammapada* (Verses and Stories), Central Institute of Higher Tibetan Studies, Sarnath, Varanasi, 1990
Encyclopaedia	:	*Encyclopaedia Britannica,* Deluxe Edition, 2001 (CD-ROM Version)
Franke	:	Franke, A.H., *Antiquities of Indian Tibet*
FrankeO	:	Franke, Otto, an article in *The Journal of the Pali text Society,* 1908
G. Tucci	:	Tucci, Giuseppe, *The Symbolism of the Temples of Bsam Yas*
Haarh	:	Erik Haarh, *The Identity of Tsu-Chih-Chien, the Tibetan king who died in 804 AD*

Contents

KS	:	Dr. Karn Singh (ed.), *Religions of India*
Lahuli	:	Lahuli, K. Angarup, former teacher in the Department of Central Asian Studies, Panjab University, Chandigarh wrote "संभोट व्याकरण" for the Hindī medium students
Lamotte	:	Lamotte, History of Indian Buddhism
Lopez	:	Lopez, Donald S. (tr.), *Religion of Tibet in Practice*
LTWA	:	Library of Tibetan Works and Archives, Dharamshala
Mullin	:	Mullin, Glenn H. (tr.), *Essence of Refined Gold* by Third Dalai Lama; Vagabond Book Inc., Delhi, 1978
Negi	:	Gangnegi, H.P., *Lo Tsa Ba Rin Chen Bzang Po and Sarma School*
Powers	:	Powers, John, *Introduction of Tibetan Buddhism*, Snow Lion Publication, NY, 1988
Prajñā	:	*Prajñādaṇḍa*, Published by University of Calcutta, 1939
Rabten	:	Rabten, Geshe: The Graduated path to Liberation.
Richardson	:	Snellgrove and Richardson, *A Cultural History of Tibet*
Ruegg	:	Ruegg, David S., *The Life of Bu-Ton Rinpoche*, 1966
SCV	:	Vidyabhushana, S.C., *A History of Indian Logic*, Motilal Banarsidass, Delhi, 1971
Shakabpa	:	Shakabpa, W.D., *A Political History of Tibet*
Shesrab	:	Shes Rab Dong Bu, contributions from Calcutta University press. A.C. Banarjee and other have done tremendous job in 1970s. Mahabyutpatti was also one of the

		most important book that was prepare in bi-lingual (Tibetan-Sanskrit) from here.
Tharchin	:	Tharchin, Geshe Lobsang, *Tsongkhapa The principle Teachings of Buddhism*
Tharchinhin	:	Self-teaching Reader for Tibetan and Indians named, "तिब्बती-हिन्दी स्वयं शिक्षक" by Geshe Tharchin published from Kalimpong in early 1963
Thupten	:	*Thbten Zepai Gyen*, Sarnath Edition, Sarnath, Varanasi, U.P. India
Tucci Rinchen	:	Tucci Giuseppe, *Rinchen Zangpo and Renaissance of Buddhism and the Millennium*
Tucci	:	Tucci, Giuseppe, *Tibetan painted Scrolls*
Tuklku	:	Tulku Dhondup
Wangyal	:	Wangyal, Geshe, *The Door of Liberation*
Warder	:	Warder, A.K., *Indian Buddhism*
Wayman	:	Wayman, Alex, *The Introduction of Buddhist Tantric Systems.*

Introduction

BUDDHISM is the third largest religious system of the world (beside Christianity and Islam at the first and second places respectively) and it is the only religious system which originated in Indian sub-continent and spread all over the world. To know the social, political and economic history of India during the time of Buddha, i.e., sixth century BC, there are several sources but to know the ideas and philosophical order of that time, we have either to rely upon the testament within the said system and the literature or that of archaeological remains which tell many ideas that can be decipherd to date. Both left the scope of interpretation and speculation which is although needed to some extent but sometimes portray a shadow over the crux of the systems of ancient era. Nevertheless, I have chosen to discuss about the two religious order of Buddhism of Tibet. The idea itself seems to be very delightful but the presence of meager resource materials often discourages a fruitful research and application of the modern research methodology. But research methodology is not only to solve the problem but quite often to raise a problem instead of solving them in order to invite further research and hence itself is called an independent research.

Tibet, one of the highest countries in the world had received Buddhism from India in seventh century AD when Padmasambhava established the monastic orders. That branch of Buddhism was known as Nyingma or the Red Hats. That was under the reign of King Songsen Gampo and the source of establishing the Buddhism was the Indian schools. Besides that, the Chinese school of sudden enlightenment, which was somewhat different from the gradual school of Indian Buddhism, also tried to establish its firm feet in the land of snow. But the Indian Buddhist *puṇḍit* defeated the Hashang, Chinese teacher of Buddhism and it was a land mark in the history of Buddhism in Tibet because this decided the way in which Tibet will follow the Buddhism in future. Though this is not highlighted in the historical record of Tibet, but this doesn't undermine its importance.

Centuries passed and the Buddhism after one persecution by the Lang Dharma, revived. The newer sects came up with fresh ideas, but the older sect (Nyingma) continued to influence not only the folk wisdom, but the aristocrats too were the followers of Nyingma sect at the time of the introduction of the Gelug sect or the Yellow Hat sect by Tsong kha Pa. In my present work, I have tired an attempt to described both Nyingma and Gelug through the eyes of modern research methodology. Side by side, I kept the descriptive ideas of the sects where it was needed to highlight the ideas of the Buddhism in the said context. But the presence of different practices itself show the comparison. At that juncture, I have taken the task of illustrating the facts only. However, I have tried to describe Buddhism in general and the two sects in particular in their full length. In the first chapter, I have dealt with the "History of Buddhism in India" which in my opinion needed more than ever because either the material available now a days gives one only an idea about how a prince of Śākya clan achieved enlightenment around 2564 years ago. Or it describes the Buddhist philosophy with all of its technicalities and that too in extol and worshipping manner. Surprisingly sometimes this attracts even the scholars from not only the non-Buddhist fields, but from the discipline itself. I have tried to be cautious while describing the ideas of the sects and therefore, I have tried to put the historical Buddha and his teaching in one chapter in a simplest possible manner that will create an interest in the mind of the Buddhist scholars and reveal the Buddha from the Tibetan point of view which is scarcely done with the use of research methodology. For this, I began with the life sketch of the prince Siddhārtha from his birth to enlightenment and then the important happenings in the life of Lord Buddha. Writing this, I tried to clarify that to whom are we calling the Buddha? A Śākya prince or the emanation of supreme God: one is historical personality who, through his penances and mortification got the way to salvation, the other one who out of his great compassion toward mankind emanates himself for the benefit of sentient beings to show them the path of freedom from all sufferings. In my opinion, here lies the difference between Mahāyāna and Sthaviravāda School of Buddhism. The former claims to be the original successor of Buddhism from sixth century BC and asserts that the way prince Siddhārtha got enlightenment; everybody can get it and become *arhat*.[1] On the other hand, the highest goal of Mahāyāna is Buddhahood and the supreme Buddha post is not achievable by a human being.

The list of Pāli canons is also given in this chapter and the name of six contemporary thinkers of Buddha is listed with their respective philosophies. Renunciation, *bodhicitta* and the Right view, these three are the base of Mahāyāna theory of Śūnyavāda or the theory of Void which originated though in India, found its firm feet in the land of snow. These points have been dealt in such a manner that while the research methodology was justified, the traditional Buddhist belief was also taken care of and even a common reader can infer the same conclusion that a Buddhist practitioner found after practising it for a long duration.

In the second chapter, I have put forth the "History of Buddhism in Tibet" with the background of the subject-matter of my book. This chapter covers the inception of Buddhism in Tibet during seventh century from the first dissemination

1. A person who becomes frees from ignorance, greed and hatred and, above all the subtle most form of defilements. This is the highest goal according to Hīnayāna that can be achieved by a practitioner.

of it up to the establishment of the Gelugpa School by Je Tsong Kha Pa. Also, I have added a short description of the history of Tibet, up to the present time, for the continuity of the subject-matter. The contents of this chapter cover the history of Buddhism chronologically. In the land of snow, it was really a Herculean task for Padmasambhava to establish Buddhism. This work can only be done by the assimilation of the local beliefs and their gods in Buddhism and Padmasambhava has successfully done so with the help of his other Indian companions like Kamalaśīla and others along with the royal patronage. A country following Shamanist practices has seen first time the logic-based religion that was most powerful and widespread at that time all over the Asia and its fragrance was across the globe. No wonder Padmasambhava is considered as second Buddha among Tibetans. The introduction of Buddhism in Tibet is linked closely with the introduction of literature as the work was started in the country by the minister of Srong Tsan Gampo, the great Thonmi Sambhota. So a brief history of Tibetan language and literature was inevitable. Therefore, I have given the Tibetan Alphabets and their Sanskrit and Roman equivalent for the record along with the historical background of the Tibetan language. Here one point I want to emphasize upon is, while writing this thesis, I faced two major difficulties: one was the Tibetan U-Chan fonts for the computer and the second the method of Romanization of Tibetan and Sanskrit words. For the first, I applied two types of U-Chan fonts namely, U-Chan TTF and L Tibetan. For the second one, I have followed the most accepted form and wherever I feel to express my ideas in either script, I did so. That is why the Romanization is not in a strict way as that of Dr. Snellgrove type with the diacritic marks or other equivalents. After this, I took the historical background of the Chinese Hashang Mahāyāna which advocates suddedn enlightenment and its clash with the Indian school of Budhism which was in favour of graduated path to salvation; this shows the reason why the graduated path is being practised in Tibet and not the Chinese counterpart of it. Then I took the destruction of Buddhism in Tibet by Lang Dharma and the resurgence of Buddhism after more than 300 years of silence/recluse. Then the Sharma Schools of thought appeared, the latest of which is Gelugpa which command good favor among the Tibetan till today. The founder of this sect was TsongkhaPa. I have put the TsongkhaPa and GelugPa in a separate chapter because of its comprehensiveness which was the demand of my research topic.

In the third chapter the "Padmasambhava and Nyingma School" has been placed with all of its possible contents. Firstly I have taken Padmasambhava and the establishment of Buddhism in Tibet, and then the main characteristics and the salient features of this school of thought were placed under the different sub-chapters.

In the fourth chapter, I have continued from the previous chapter about Nyingmas and dealt with their practices through which they are known. Therefore I name it after one of the greatest and famous practice, Dzogchen. Hence the chapter is named as, "Terton and other practices in Nyingma." Because of the innate nature of Nyingma sect to adopt Tāntric practices, I have tried to put light on the Tāntric practice specially.

After this, in a short chapter, I have tried to explain why the sectarian tendencies came out from a disciplined system like Buddhism that is considered to be the most logical and scientific in its approach. The content of this chapter, though very short in the number of pages, carry very high value to understand the birth of an ism within the ism. Though I have named it, "Emergence of Schism in Buddhism," but in this chapter some other general topics were also covered which are the answers to the curiosities in the field of Tibetan Buddhism. For example, I have given a very brief account of the translation work of the Tibetan literature in Tibet and after 1959, in India and abroad.

In the sixth chapter, namely "TsongkhaPa and the Gelugpa

school fo Tibet," I have given the salient features and practices of the sect. Why the actual need to establish this sect was felt by its founder TsongkhaPa when he had already mastered all the then time philosophies through other prevalent sects. The role of Rendawa in the educational and philosophical life of TsongkhaPa is evident in all the literature, which TsongkhaPa wrote. In fact, when we go through the ascetic life of TsongkhaPa, he seems to be much more powerful, when his name became famous than himself, than what he was in his settled life. Wandering in the search of knowledge through debates, asking every established master to impart knowledge, doing penances, these all create a gamut around TsongkhaPa's personality that every researcher inspire for. This is more relevant today when we see the education has become a means nothing more than for earning the bread. Also, the followers of TsongkhaPa (with due respect) have indulged themselves in the very politics, which TsongkhaPa had forbid in his lifetime.

The content of the GelugPa School needed more elaborate study to discuss, so I divided it into two chapters and the chapter eighth in its succession, I have tried to highlight the philosophy and ethics of GelugPas, which they are famous for. I named this chapter "The stages of path and other teachings of GelugPa." The biggest contribution in this regard was the Lam Rim teachings, by the founder of this sect, TsongkhaPa. TosongkhaPa during his study time engaged in debate with almost all the teacher of prevalent school of Buddhism in Tibet, and found that debates are the best way to develop the intellect of a person. So he stressed very much on study of the books in his Order and hence started the tradition of Lam-Rim teachings. He himself worte a big volume named Lam-Rim Chen-Mo and tried to put all the philosophical teachings of Buddha which were required to lead a sanctimonious and virtuous life according to Vinaya. When he found the book to be too voluminous to remember, he prepared a précis form of the book and named it Lam-Tso Nam Sum (ལམ་གཙོ་རྣམ་གསུམ) which became so famous that the

Gelugpa or the yellow hats were sometime called the followers of Lam Tso Nam Sum. I have tried to brief the teaching content of Lam Tso Nam Sum in this chapter. In addition, I have given, at the end of this chapter, why the Prasangika Madhyamika (དབུ་མ་ཐལ་འགྱུར་པ།) has an upper hand not only over the other three main school of Buddhism[2] but over the Svatantrika Mādhyamika (དབུ་མ་རང་རྒྱུད་པ།) too.

The eighth and the final chapter is conclusion where the findings of the research work have been stated.

Finally, I want to quote a verse from the Dhammapada which describes the Buddhasasana or the law of Buddha, with the presupposition that if this verse is being taken care of, be it any sect or sub-sect of Buddhism anywhere at the globe, the Buddhism will succeed in achieving its goal.

सब्ब पापस्स अकरणं, कुसलस्स उपसम्पदा।
सचित्त परियोदपन्नं, एतान् बुद्धां सासनं ॥183॥

Abstinence from all evil, Fulfilment of all good
Purification of one's mind, This is the law of Buddha.[3]

---

2. The three other schools of Buddhism are: (1) Vaibhāṣikas (2) Sautrāntikas and (3) Vijñānavādins or Yogācāra.
3. *The Religions of India*, Preface, ed. Dr. Karn Singh.

1

Buddhism in India

THE sixth century BC has great importance in the history of social and cultural reforms throughout the world. The whole world witnessed the emergence of new religious teachers. The demand of the time was to find new ways to answer religious inquisitions. The main reason behind that was the obsolete and trite methodologies to quench the intellectual enquiries of the societies. So the sixth century BC was remarkable for the spiritual unrest and intellectual ferment all over the globe. In China we find Lao Tzu and Confucius; in Greece Parmenides and Empedocles, in Iran Zarathustra, in India Mahāvīra and the Buddha.[1] The light which the Buddha showed us is also lit well outside India. Tibet and Sri Lanka are the two countries which are the proven reservoirs of Buddhist teaching since ages. Sri Lanka has got importance for the revival of Hīnayāna teachings and Tibet for the Mahāyāna teachings.

The religion of Tibet has long been an object of fascination for all over the world. Tibet, is called Shangri-La[2] by the Western scholars. From the time since Venetian travellers

---

1. In addition to that, Pāli sources describe six contemporary thinkers of Buddha namely, Pūraṇakaśyapa, Makkhali Ghoṣāla, Ajitakeśakambali, Pakudh Kātyāyana, Sañjaya Velatthiputra, Nighaṇṭhanāthaputra, etc., in *Sāmānyaphala Sutta* of *Dīgh Nikāya* in *Sutta Piṭaka*.

2. An imaginative place described only in literature and stories where the youth of a person lasts forever.

and Catholic missionaries encountered Tibetan monks at the Mongol court, tales of mysteries of their mountain homeland and the magic of their strange religions have held European and American imaginations in a peculiar awe. On the other hand, India has a very long history of Indo-Tibet relationship. Therefore, in the eyes of India, Tibet is different. According to the centuries old traditions and also quoted by the present Dalai Lama Tenzin Gyatso,

> Tibet always looks forward to India as India is his Guru. The relationship of Teacher-taught still beats the heart of Tibetan religious system since long. Over the past two centuries, the valuation of Tibetan society and, particularly its religion has fluctuated wildly.

Tibetan Buddhism has been portrayed sometimes as the most corrupt deviation from the Buddha's true *dharma*, sometimes, as its most direct descendant.[3]

Indian tradition maintains the Buddha as the ninth and latest incarnation of Lord Viṣṇu. On the other hand, Mahāyāna Buddhism (only Mahāyāna is in practice in Tibet) maintains Buddha as an eternal super mundane God and Viṣṇu, Indra and others gods as deities subject to every suffering and happiness as other beings.

In the light of above facts, being a student of Buddhist studies, I began to research and examine the religion and philosophy of Tibet as such. My Tibetan teacher Prof. G.G. Gyatso guided me and helped a lot to understand the Tibetan culture and religious system. As soon as I came closer to Tibetan societies, the similarities and dissimilarities opened my eyes wider and wider.

The present work is an attempt to understand the Buddhism of Tibet with all its variations of sects and sub-sects within Buddhism (ནང་ཆོས།) "Sangye kyi Chos" where Sangye means Buddha in Tibetan language) and this, with

3. Lopez.

special reference to their roots in the land of their origin (India). Nowadays every practice by Tibetan Lamas is being watched by us in a strange manner and with the approach in mind that it is a foreign practice. Their prayer wheel, engraved Tibetan spells on the rocks Hand drums (*ḍamaru*) and many more things look like peculiar cult-objects. Nevertheless, in reality, they have their origin in India. As we come across the Himālayan regions of India the scene of live Buddhist societies can be seen everywhere.

Tibetan Buddhism

Buddhism in Tibet has very deep roots in the Indian history, culture, literature and social patterns. Nothing than this, lone fact can prove my supposition right that until date when the temporal head of Tibet, Dalai Lama dies, his head turn after sometime towards India. The Tibetan traditional system says that it is in order to seek the blessings from the place where Siddhārtha got enlightenment and became Buddha (present Gayā city in Bihar). So in order to under-stand Buddhism of Tibet, we must understand the Buddhism of India along with the social, political, cultural and religious awakenings of Indian masses. The study of circumstances and conditions of India in sixth century BC and prerequisites of establishing a new way of life which the modern world know as Buddhism, is a must to know Buddhism totaly. It is necessary to describe the life and happenings of the founder of Buddhism and to compare his life-study to that of the founders of Buddhism in Tibet.

Life of Buddha

PRINCE SIDDHĀRTHA

About the birth of Buddha, the resource book is *Lalitavistara* in Pāli. Buddha, prior to be known as Buddha was named prince Siddhārtha. He was born in the royal family of Gautama of Kapilvastu near the plains of Indo-Nepal border geogra-phically in West Bengal.[4] His father was Śuddhodana who was chief of Śākya clan and was the designated king. Siddhārtha's mother was Māyā Devī (Mahāmāyā). Several references have been given of the birth year of prince Siddhārtha but most widely acceptable of them is 483 BC. When Māyā Devī was pregnant, she dreamt a white flying elephant entering into her womb.

Next morning, the interpretation of that dream was the subject-matter of the royal court of Śuddhodana. The royal astrologer[5] revealed the meaning and said that the dream was the pre-information of taking birth of an extraordinary personality. In due course of time when the time of pregnancy matured, Māyā Devī gave birth to a boy child. At the time of delivery, she was on route to her parental home. The birth of the child took place near Lumbinī in a garden at the midst of two *sāla* trees. The future prospect of the child was the concern for both Śuddhodana and Māyā Devī. Therefore, once again the royal astrologer was consulted. The interpretation of the astrologer was an unusual one. He came with the opinion that either the boy will become a *cakravartin* (all-sovereign) king or a great sage. King Śuddhodana's choice was traditional one. So he wanted[6] his son to become an all-sovereign king only and accordingly he made all the arrangement to the boy in his upbringing like a king. He commanded his men to take all the precaution so that the boy prince could not be exposed to any kind of sorrow or misery or to see any kind of unpleasant scene. All types of luxurious things piled around the prince. In spite

---

4. Auboyer, Delhi, 1983, pp 23. Some Indian scholars recognize the place of birth of Buddha as Lumbiṇī near Piprahava in district Bastī of UP.

5. Depicted in Buddhist scriptures (*Lalitavistara*) as sage named Asita, the non-Buddhist literature named him as *Kāla-Devala*.

6. In Buddhist terminology, it means giving up the desire for the material world and ready to proceed to the path of salvation. Technically known as ངགཏ

of all, if one believes the stories, Siddhārtha was sensitized to unhappiness and difficulties though he had no personal knowledge of them, since he had been carefully protected from such mishaps.

YOUNG AGE AND MARRIAGE

Thus, the prince was brought up in an exemplary luxurious environment and in due time, got married with a princess Yaśodharā. In due course of time, she gave birth to a boy and he was named Rāhula. Now the long awaited time came which turned the history as the becoming of a great person had to take place.

Renunciation

ENCOUNTER WITH SUFFERING

The prince Siddhārtha used to go on evening walks with his charioteer friend Caṇḍaka. Once he met a sick person during his walk. The sick person was in pitiable condition and crying with pain. Flies were sticking around his wounds and the man was looking all-round for help. Prince has never come across such situations and he did not recognize what the scene was. He had never met a sick in his life time. So out of curiosity he questioned Caṇḍaka who he was. Caṇḍaka replied that everybody on this earth can fall sick and there is no way out.

Next time, when the prince was on his way to his evening walk as usual, he encountered an old man. The situation of that old man was pitiable. He was unable to walk properly having a stick in his hand for support to stand. He was in deep anguish and disquiet. Nobody was paying attention to him. His family seemed to be unresponsive in his problems. This situation was also new for prince Siddhārtha. Again, he sought an explanation from the Caṇḍaka, his friend-charioteer. Caṇḍaka replied that the old age is an inevitable part of human life and everybody will become old after his young age is gone. Siddhārtha counter questioned that whether he too, will become old or not. Caṇḍaka nodded his head in affirmation. This answer stirred his peace of mind and he then began to think that all the luxury and expediency he is availing will be fading away after sometime and he will be like the old and sick men soon.

Next time, when he was on evening walk a corpse was leading on him, on its last journey. Prince has never seen a dead body before. When he questioned Caṇḍaka that why this body is lying and where these men are taking this body, then Caṇḍaka replied that this is the truth of all human and other beings. Whosoever is born will perish sometimes. The one who is born is subject to death and this rule is unalterable and eternal, nobody on the earth has so far been able to escape from this rule. Death is certain. The prince became very uneasy and apprehensive about the conveniences and possessions.

Turning Point

THE RECLUSE

Next time, he saw a young hermit who was on his way to collect alms food. His face was shining and he seemed very cheerful and happy. The worldly sufferings seem to passed him untouched. Prince enquired Caṇḍaka about the reason for his happiness and cheer. Caṇḍaka replied that the recluse had left his household life and is in the path of salvation. He thinks for the welfare of all human beings. Because he has no desire for himself and does everything for the benefit of all, he is happy.

The meeting of above four different kinds of people were proved to be the turning point in the mind of prince Siddhārtha. He, who was always among the best, ate tasty and delicious food, enjoyed all good scents, wore best suited cloths and availed all possible kind of luxury, passed his time among beautiful girls, now saw the real and another part of life which was true and binding. He was now forced to think that one-day this all possession will not be with him and he will have to give up them. The prince somehow realized a way out of suffering though he was not a practitioner of it.

Now he made up his mind to pursue the life of happiness and find the way out of the sickness, old age and death.

The Spark

THE PARTY

The renunciation was taking place in his mind. But still he was in favour of using the things in a long lasting way and not forgetting them. He has seen the other part of life, which was the universal truth but he has not seen the ugly part of the so-called beautiful life. The spark that is essential to give up the lust for the worldly possessions was yet to be started in his life. The spark as we know come from the place where it is not expected. Therefore, that time came. The venue was a dance-drink party organized by the king Śuddhodana who has noticed the diminishing interest of his son in mundane affairs. When the party was over late in night, all the dancers and other artists after having drunk lay here and there on the floor and were soon in a deep sleep. The prince awoke early in the morning as usual and saw the beautiful bodies of the performers' lying here and there. In the state of mind, which he had, he was morbidly repelled: these sleeping women appeared to him as dead, deprived of spirit, as in some kind of pre-figuration of a funeral site. The *Lalitavistara* describes the scene as he saw it. Some of these unconscious women are drooling, yawning, snoring; others dishevelled, messy, gnash their teeth, pant, and babble senselessly. In brief, they offered the most degrading view of human nature when it is uncontrolled. The clothes of dancer girls' were half open and the otherwise hidden parts of their body were exhibited in a preposterous manner. Saliva was coming out from the mouths of some of them. Some of them were snorting badly. The whole scenario of the area was horrible and very embarrassing. This scene had acted as a spark in the thought of the Siddhārtha for renunciation and he made up his mind finally to give up the household life and proceed in the search of truth of the life which must be free from these suffering.

He started thinking how to get rid of these problems of human life. Until that time he had in his mind to get rid of their suffering and the only way out of suffering which he knew, was the shining face of hermit. At that time he only knew that the hermit was happy because he was not associated with the phenomenon world, with desire and after renouncing the worldly belonging, was in the path of God. This was the only thought, all-pervading and absolute which prince Siddhārtha can think to start his spiritual journey with.

Renunciation

So, one night leaving the royal palace, his wife and son sleeping behind, he went to further his one point mission — the search of the way that can lead him to the eternal happiness. He took with him Caṇḍaka to drive the chariot only up to the border of the kingdom. There, on the bank of the forest he alighted from the chariot, cropped his long hair with his royal sword, took his royal dress off and after donning the rags, proceeded towards the journey which culminated in the metamorphosis of Prince Siddhārtha into Lord Buddha.

Finding the way

THE AUSTERITIES

Prince Siddhārtha on his journey towards finding the way to the cessation of suffering, met various religious leaders, underwent many severe penances. He had already seen and led the life of self-enjoyment. Now he had the choice of passing through another extreme of the life, i.e., of self-mortification.

However, both the life of self-enjoyment and of self-mortification could not bring him the virtue which he was searching. He found the way, finally, at Gayā at the bank of river Nirañjana.

WANDERING

At the age of 29, he had left his royal home in search of well-being of all. He spent about seven years wandering in the search of his goal. Changing places and spiritual masters. No one could satisfy him; none of the founded way attracted him to follow. Whatever the masters suggested, he did so, but all went futile. The truth was yet ahead of him.

Enlightenment

AT BODH-GAYĀ

While doing penances, his body became weaker and weaker day by day. He was not able to move and perform normal movements. He now realizes, that neither the life of enjoyment and materialism could give you satisfaction, nor would torturing your body, lead you somewhere.

That time he was on the bank of River Nirañjana in a place near Gayā. Now he decided to nourish his body minimum to bear the hardship of meditation and perform normal duties. But that time his body was so weak that he was unable to move in the search of any kind of food.

At this very juncture, a young village girl named Sujātā (some sources name her Rādhā) gave him a sweet dish made up of rice and milk (porridge) and made him eat with her own hand because Siddhārtha was unable to do it himself. Taking the porridge, Siddhārtha now became able to move himself. He then felt vigour and new vitality in his body and new freshness in his mind. Then after re-energizing himself, he became determined more than ever to get his goal of salvation. Then he decide to do deep meditation to achieve the goal, he than sat in meditative posture and promised himself that either he will get enlightenment or perish.

BODHI, NIBBĀNA, SALVATION, ENLIGHTENMENT

Now it is very important to jot down about the enlightenment of prince Siddhārtha. What prince got under the banyan tree at Bodh-Gayā on the bank of River Nirañjana? What actually he realized? What made him Buddha from Siddhārtha, given to wandering? The true essence of Buddhism lies in the answers of these questions. The crux of salvation lies in the total mental outcome and realization along with the understanding of Siddhārtha since long. In the following pages I will try to describe what salvation is and how Gautama realized it. What actually *nibbāna, nirvāṇa* or *mokṣa* mean? What are the true teachings of Buddhism? Can it be communicated through words or we can only insinuate it through gestures and suggestive words as some scholars suspect?

Answer to these questions is not a simple one. As Buddhism through ages and also many scholars and *puṇḍit*s have contributed their valuable scholarly works, interpreting the meaning of the words told by Buddha in his 45 years long sojourn at different places in different context. However, with the help of the understanding given by my teachers I will try to reproduce it in forthcoming pages in simplest possible manner.

EVENT

Every detail has been given in Pāli, Sanskrit and Tibetan sources about the event of enlightenment that Siddhārtha got that night. Here I am bringing them in my own words in shortest possible words.

After doing austerities for six (or seven) years, Buddha realized that it leads nowhere and the weakened body will be unable to engage itself in meditation enthusiastically, so he decided to nourish his body minimum. That time a nearby girl who was with her cows there offered him the sweet rice porridge which gave Siddhārtha renewed energy and vitality, which enlivened him to more ahead in his search via meditation. The Māra (the Satan of Buddhism) caused all possible hindrances in the way of Siddhārtha in order to deviate him from his meditation. He sent demons and other devil creatures to prevent Gautama's ascension to attain Buddhahood.

However, non of these could shape the firm resolve of steadfast Siddhārtha and he continued non-deviated in his meditation. Then Māra sent his daughters to seduce prince Siddhārtha. Nevertheless, they also failed to disturb the concentration of Gautama. After defeating Māra, Siddhārtha proclaimed that either I will attain enlightenment or will perish. He attained the *bodhi*.

BODHI

In the first watch of night[7] Siddhārtha realized the law of action and result. In the second watch of night, he acquired "Three knowledge's (རིག་པ་གསུམ)." He came to know his all previous births, comprehended four Noble Truths and how sentient beings transmigrate in accordance with law of action (*karma*, ལས). In the third watch of night, he realized cause of suffering and the way it can be eliminated.

At dawn, he perfected his awareness[8] and became a Buddha. A being who has eliminated even the subtle most traces of ignorance, who has become omniscience and spontaneously, perfectly passionate.

Then Buddha, knowing that his knowledge surpasses all mundane wisdom, no one on this earth will be able to understand this knowledge. Therefore, whether it should be given to sentient beings or not, he became dual minded. But after several weeks of thinking in the state of transcendent meditation, it was his great compassion for the beings that dominated over all other thoughts and apprehensions and finally he decided to devote himself to teach his realization to the people so might they became free from suffering.

---

7. According to Buddhist masters, *nirvāṇa* is a state of mind which is beyond description. Late Prof. Mahesh Tiwari (one of my teacher at university of Delhi) was of the opinion that whosoever has experience even the slightest taste of that state, will be unable to communicate it.

8. A watch or *ghaḍī* is a unit of time in ancient Indian equivalent to one hour and 30 minutes.

Spread of Buddhism

PRATHAM DHARMACAKRAPRAVARTANA

When Buddha finally decided to dessiminate his realization of enlightenment to entire sentient beings;[9] he then began his teaching at Sārnāth where he met, five ascetics, who were his previous companions while Buddha was wandering in the search of truth. Buddha gave his first sermon at the deer park in Sārnāth (near Vārāṇasī in UP). After some suspicion and hesitation, when they were satisfied with the Buddha's achievements, all the five companions of his previous time became his first five followers. This is known in the world as "Turning the First wheel of law into motion" དང་པོ་ཆོས་ཀྱི་འཁོར་ལོ་འཁྱུར་བ། or *pratham dharmacakrapravartana.* Then Kauṇḍinya, one among first five ascetics, realized the knowledge and became the First *arhat* (དགྲ་བཅོམ་པ།) in Buddhism. An *arhat* is the one who will attain *nirvāṇa* at the end of the present life as a result of elimination of all phenomenon defilements (three defilements are basic defilements, Attachment, Hatred and Jealousy in Tibetan འདོད་ཆགས་ཞེ་སྡང་དང་གཏིགས་མག།). Then these five ascetics asked Buddha to be accepted by him as his disciples formally.

Then Buddha asked them to take refuge in *dharma* and in Buddha (*saṅgha*, was yet to be established). After rainy season, Buddha began to travel that is called *carīka* that he did for as many as 45 years till his death in 567 BC. So Buddha began his *carīka*, teaching people with his deep knowledge

---

9. It is written in the scriptures that after getting enlightenment, Buddha declared himself as an aware person knowing the reasons which make a being live in *saṁsāra* and announced that he will not come as in the bondage as usually an ordinary person take birth in this phenomenal world. The following verse is taken for reference from the Pāli *Dhammapada*: verse no. 154:

   गहकारक दिठ्ठोसि । पुन गेहं न काहसि ।
   सब्बा ते फासुका भग्गा । गहकूटं विसंखतं ।
   विसंखारगतं चित्तं । तण्हानं खयमज्झगा ॥

and insight, the wisdom and the middle path which he had discovered. During Buddha's time, according to Tibetan sources and also Pāli scriptures, we come across the names of six great spiritual leaders whom Buddha defeated. In the following pages the name and philosophies of those six great thinkers are given in nutshell.

Six Contemporary Thinkers of Buddha
ལུ་སྟེགས་ཅན་གྱི་སྟོན་པ་དྲུག་གི་མིང་།

The name of the thinkers and their philosophies as given in *Sāmānyaphala Sutta* of *Dīgha Nikāya* in *Sutta Piṭaka* (the collection of the words of Buddha) is as follows:

PŪRAṆAKAŚYAPA (OD SUNG DZOG BYED འོད་སྲུང་རྫོགས་བྱེད།)

Pūraṇakaśyapa or Pūranakassappa was the profounder of *akriyāvāda* or No-Action Theory. According to him there is no action, which brings sin or merit. There is no good result of good action or bad result of bad action.

MAKKHALIGOSĀLA (KUNTU GYU NE LHE KYI BU ཀུན་ཏུ་རྒྱུ་གནས་ལྷས་ཀྱི་བུ།)

This spiritual leader had very commanding status in the society. He had large number of followers. His philosophy is known as *niyativāda* or predestine. According to him, there is no relation between action and result. There is neither doer nor doing. The suffering or happiness to anybody is just a matter of chance. So, like the ball of cotton when by projectile force goes upside and after diminishing the projectile force comes back, in the same way the sorrow of the human being will be vanished. It can be said that the philosophy of Makkhaligosāla is not a logical one because according to him there is no logical relation between the action and result.

AJITKEŚAKAMBALA (མི་ཕམ་སྐྲུཡི་ལ་བ་ཅན།)

Ajitkeśakambala or Ajitakeśakambali has very large number of followers. He had very long hairs and they cover whole of his body, hence, he got his name. His philosophy is called *ucchedvāda* or Nihilism. According to him, there is neither heaven nor hell. Man is composed of four elements and when he or she dies earth element goes to greater earth and air, fire and water elements vanished into the sky. And there is no soul or such thing that carry result of *karma*. There is no life after death.

PRAKUDH KĀTYĀYANA (ཀཙུའི་བུ་རོག་ཅན།)

Prakudh Kātyāyana or Pakudhkaccāna had also very large number of followers. He too, had commanding position in the society. His philosophy can be named as *akṛtavāda* or *satkāyavāda*. His theory seem that there is no relation between action and its result. According to him, the whole universe in made of seven components, viz., earth, fire, water, air, happiness, sorrow, and life. Neither they affect each other nor do they have any effect or action in the life of any being. So, there is no action and also there is none who is doing any action.

NIGAṆṬHNĀTH PUTTA (གཅེར་བུ་པ་གཉེན་གྱི་བུ།)

This spiritual leader is said to be the Jain *tīrthaṁkara* by many historian who got defeated by the Buddha. He, like the Jain *tīrthaṁkara* was advocating the theory of *cāturyāma saṁvara*. According to him, the follower of his path is that of *nirgantha* and he is supposed to adorn with the four *saṁvara*s. They are: Of behaviour with water so that the beings in water won't die, devoid of all sins, of the result of devoid of all sins and finally engaged in removing all such sins.

SAÑJAYAVELLATHI PUTTA (སྨྲ་འདོད་ཀྱི་བུ་མོའི་བུ་ཡང་དག་རྒྱལ་བ་ཅན།)

This philosopher seems to be a typical confused one. His philosophy is termed as *vicchedavāda* or negation of all affirmation of none. He had taken the view to negate all supposition and not to establish any statement of his own. He used to say that He neither affirm nor deny the existence of heaven or hell or any pre-suppositions that is prevalent there. Neither was he saying this, nor that. So, in my opinion he rather seems to be advocating silence but not no-action. He seems to be in favour of being aloof from any action. This thing may be, may not be. There may be heaven or hell or there may not be.

Methodology of Buddha

BUDDHA AS PHYSICIAN

Buddha never advocated for himself that he is propagating a new religious system or religion. He used to say that he was giving a new way of life to lead. In that way Lord Buddha emerged as a physician, who cured all the ailments of the past, present and future lives. Tradition told us one name of Buddha is Bhaiṣajya Guru or the Buddha of medicine. The followers of six contemporary thinkers came to Buddha along with others and became his disciples.

DIALECTIC METHOD

It is noteworthy that Buddha taught everyone who came and asked for it. He never attempted to attract people into his new order or he never tried to formulate a new religion. As A.K. Warder has noted,

> It is most characteristic of Buddha that he always adapts his talk to the person he is conversing with. His courtesy in argument resulted from this: it is certainly not his way to denounce the opinions and practice of another to his face and challenge him to justify them. His method rather is to seem to adopt the other's point of view and than by question and answer to improve it until a position compatible with his own has been arrived at. Thus he leads his partner in discussion towards the truth as he has discovered it, but so that the partner seems himself to continue his own quest, in whatever form he had taken, and to arrive at higher truth he had previously been aware of, or more convincing moral ideas.[10]

---

10. Warder, pp. 64-65.

The Teachings of Buddha

BUDDHISM IN DIFFERENT PLACES

We found difference in the teachings of Buddha from different sources now a days. Buddhism was patronized by the great Indian kings like Aśoka and also by foreign invaders who became kings of Indian territories such as Kaniṣka. As we find Buddhism now in different countries with sects and sub-sects of local and Indian origin.

In China, the Mahāyāna is prominent. In Tibet and Japan also Mahāyāna has developed with its root in local soil, but they also develop local version as Vajrayāna in Tibet and Zen Buddhism in Japan as their special area with local influences and interpretation; though the basic teachings of Buddha remained the same. One more thing is noteworthy. As far as 18 countries in the world can be counted to be more or less Buddhist countries and numerically, every fourth person of the world is Buddhist.[11]

TRANSLATIONS

Every country has translated the teaching of the master to enable its men to follow the path with easiness in the communicative words in the native language, but the translation work of Tibet is considered to be the most authentic and closest to the original one in the world of Mahāyāna Buddhism. So, in the light of Pāli sources as well as Tibetan and Sanskrit translation, I will try to reproduce the teaching of Lord in nearest possible manner in which the word of Buddha's saying must be.

The collections of Teachings

PĀLI LITERATURE

The whole Pāli literature is divided into two classes, viz., the literature in *Tripiṭakas* and the literature outside the *Tripiṭakas*.

---

11. *KS*, Introduction.

Here the context is only to the classic literature of *Tripiṭakas*. The complete list of Pāli canon along with the literature outside the *Tripiṭaka* is given at the end.

TRIPIṬAKAS

The teachings of Buddha as found in Pāli today are more or less restored from the Sri Lanka's collection of teachings. However according to Pāli sources, the teachings are divided into three baskets called *Piṭakas*: the following table is given to summarise the contents of the three *Piṭakas*:

Vinaya Piṭaka	*Sutta Piṭaka*	*Abhidhamma Piṭaka*
Collection of the Discourses: pertaining to the rules regarding monks and nuns.	The collection of saying of the Buddh : About religion as general to all.	Collection of the commentaries of Buddhist scholars given by them from time to time. It is higher philosophical interpretation of religion and can be compared to Upaniṣads as far as subject-matter is concern.

Vinaya Piṭaka is divided into three categories: *Sutta, Vibhaṅga* or *Pātimokkha*

It has two sub-divisions in it namely (a) Bhikkhu Pātimokkha and (b) Bhikkhunī Pātimokkha.

Khandaka: It has also two sub-divisions as (a) Mahāvagga and, (b) Chullavagga.

Parivār: Collection of laws of monks and nuns and their historical prospects.

Sutta Piṭaka is divided into five categories called *Nikāyas*. They are: (a) *Dīgha Nikāya*, (b) *Majjhima Nikāya*, (c) *Saṁyutta Nikāya*, (d) *Anyukta Nikāya*, and (e) *Khuddaka Nikāya*

The famous 423 stories of *Dhammapada* and nearly 550 stories of *Jātakas* are also parts of the *Sutta Piṭaka*.

Abhidhamma Piṭaka: It is the collection of higher philosophical text by Buddhist scholars. It comprises of seven books. They are as following:

Puggalapañati: It describes various kinds of beings and it also deal with the philosophy of mind.

Dhātu-Kathā: It tells us about the various components and its subjects of sentient beings.

Dhamma Sangiṇī: It describes various states of mind and its subsidiaries.

Vibhaṅga: It is also a supplementary book of *Dhamma Saṅgiṇī*, which is given number one position in *Abhidhamma Piṭaka*. It also gives us various aspects of knowledge.

Patthanpakaraṇa: This is the biggest and the most complex book of *Abhidhamma Piṭaka*. We found 24 types of *Pacchaya* (*Pratyaya*-relativity) in this book.

Kathāvatthu: It describes the history of Buddhist religion. It is believed to be the creation of Moggaliputta Tissa.

Yamaka: This briefly deals with logical discussion whether "this" is "this" or "that," etc.

Kanjur and Tanjur: The Collection of the Teachings of Buddha in Tibet

སྡེ་སྣོད་གསུམ་དང་བཀའ་འགྱུར་དང་བསྟན་འགྱུར།

The above list of Buddhist canon was divided into three collections collectively called *Tripiṭaka* or the three boxes (of teachings). The above collection is from Pāli side which is of course *Sthaviravāda* or commonly known as Hīnayāna. Pāli was the language of common people of the parts of Bihar and surrounding areas during sixth century BC where Buddha usually sojourned. But there is other form of Buddhism, Mahāyāna which Tibet follows. From the Tibetan side, though we came to know about the name of *Tripiṭaka*s (སྡེ་སྣོད་གསུམ) but they have their own Tibetan division of the teaching of Lord Buddha, divided into two categories only. The first one, which is the collection of the sayings of Buddha, is called *Kanjur* (བཀའ་གྱུར།) and the second collection is called *Tanjur* (བསྟན་འགྱུར), which is collection of the treatises of the Buddhist *puṇḍits* and *ācārya*s including their commentaries too.

Here it is not less important to mention that the Tibetan *Kanjur*, which is the collection of Buddha's sayings, included some of the excellent Tibetan and Indian works too. The reason behind it as told by my teacher Tibetan Lama Prof. Gyatso is that Buddhism in Tibet came directly from India without any medium and from India they came to know about the teacher-taught relationship. According to tradition of India and Tibet the works of Indian and Tibetan masters were considered to be equivalent to the Buddha's words itself. I am giving a brief account of the division of Tibetan Buddhist cannon as I found in the reference books:

Kanjur (བཀའ་འགྱུར།) is divided into nine categories of books; each category has further sub-categories of books:

1. འདུལ་བ། ***or the Vinaya Texts*** — The seven books under these categories deal with the rules pertaining to monks and nuns. It gives us the description of the Buddhist councils also.
2. ཤེར་ཕྱིན།. ***or the Prajñāpāramitā*** — The full name of this category is ཤེས་རབ་ཀྱི་ཕ་རོལ་ཏུ་ཕྱིན་པ།, it has thirty-six books in its category.
3. ཕལ་ཆེན། ***or Avataṁsakas*** — It has only one book in its category.
4. དཀོན་བརྩེགས ***or Ratnakūṭa*** — It comprises forty-nine books in it.
5. མདོ་སྡེ ***or Sutrānta*** — It has large collection of two hundred and sixty-six books in it.
6. རྒྱུད་འབུམ། ***or the Tantra*** — Unlike Pāli canon, Tibetan tradition believes that Tantra is a part of *Buddhavacana* or the sayings of the Buddha and the chief exponent of Tantra is Padmasambhava, who is considered in Tibetan Buddhism as Buddha of Tantra. It has four hundred and sixty eight books in its collection.
7. རྙིང་རྒྱུད།. ***or the Old Tantra*** — It has seventeen books and some of the pre-Buddhist tradition can be seen in it.

8. དུས་འཁོར།. ***or the Kalcakra Tantra*** — It has only one book and the Buddha of compassion is authorized exponent of it.

9. གཟུངས་འདུས། ***or the Mantra Saṁgraha*** — It comprises of two hundred and sixty three books and is one of the biggest collections of magic spells in the religion.

Now, the details of བསྟན་འགྱུར། ***Tanjur*** — *Tanjur* is divided into seventeen sub categories, which are further divided into categories of books.

1. བསྟོད་ཚོགས ***or the Strotra*** — It has seventy-one books in its category.

2. རྒྱུད ***or the Tantra*** — As given in Tibetan sources, it seems to be the biggest collection of Tāntric books. It comprises of two thousand six hundred and six books. I came across some of the books and am of the view, my Tibetan teacher also share my view, that most of these books have been taken from various Tāntric systems and beliefs available in Indian sub-continent.

3. ཤེར་ཕྱིན། or ཤེས་རབ་ཀྱི་ཕ་རོལ་ཏུ་ཕྱིན་པ།. ***or Prajñāparāmitā Sūtra*** — In this category there are thirty-eight books.

4. དབུ་མ ***or Mādhyamika*** — It has one hundred and fifty seven books in it.

5. མདོ་འགྲེལ ***or Sūtra Ṭīkā*** — As evident from name it is the collection of various commentaries given by Indian *puṇḍits* on the words of Buddha. There are thirty-nine books in it.

6. སེམས་ཙམ།. ***or Yogācāra*** — There is a sect in Buddhist philosophy by this name. But here this means the book that gives us an account of Yoga and its philosophies.

7. མངོན་པ།. ***or Abhidharma*** — We can put these books in *Abhidharma Piṭaka* of Pāli Canon. It comprises higher philosophy of Buddhism in India and Tibet but has more books than Pāli tradition have. It has eighteen books unlike only seven in Pāli of same category.

8. འདུལ་བ།. *or Vinaya* — It has forty-six books in it.

9. སྐྱེས་རབས།. *or Jātakas* — The Pāli tradition does not count *Jātaka*s as part of *Tripiṭaka* though it is very much a part of Pāli canon.

10. སྤྲིང་ཡིག།. *or Letters* — It comprises forty-five books. One of the famous books among these forty-five is the letter written by the great Buddhist master of Nālandā, Nāgārjuna to the king Gotamīputra.

11. ཚད་མ།. *or the Pramāṇa Śāstra* — It comprises sixty-six books.

12. སྒྲ་མདོ།. *or Grammar or Śabda Śāstra* — It has thirty-seven books in it.

13. གསོ་བ་རིག་པ།. *or Cikitsā Śāstra* — In this Tibetan tradition it is mentioned that the Buddha is the ultimate doctor who can cure our all mental, physical, psychological and all other problems. So they believe that Buddha is our master of medicine (Bhaiṣajya Guru) and Buddha himself gives every medicine on this earth, herbs, etc., and their method of preparation.

14. བཟོ་རིག་པ། *or Śilpa Vidyā* — It has given us how to sketch *maṇḍala, dhāriṇī* and other Tāntric diagrams. It also provides us the geometry of *pagoḍā*s. It has fifteen books in it.

15. ཐུན་མོང་བ་ལུགས་ཀྱི་བསྟན་བཅོས། *or Samaya Śāstra* — It has eighteen books in it.

16. སྣ་ཚོགས། *or Miscellaneous* — Those books which were not covered under any strict category and are of general nature are collected under this category. It comprises of one hundred and nineteen books.

17. ཇོ་བོའི་ཆོས་ཆུང་། *or the Books written by Atiśa* — Under this category there are one hundred and three books.

2

Buddhism in Tibet

TIBET, the land of Lāmās, Yāks and centre of several mystical stories is considered Shangri-La of East the place of eternal youth. Because it remained closed to Western society and outer world until 1959, the final and successful Chinese attack, seldom anybody from west knew anything truth about it.

Starting from its nomenclature, the native of Tibet called their country Bod (བོད). Most probably, the name Tibet has been derived from Mongolian word Thubet. But one most convincing suggestion according to me and I suppose to which the scholar community have the word of affirmation in this regard is that, the word Tibet is derived from the Sanskrit word Triviṣṭapa which we found in the Kālidāsa's work, used for Tibet (heaven). It seems logical that in due course of time, *tri* became Ti and *vṛṣṭapa* converted into Bet.

To understand Tibet and Buddhism of Tibet, a clear distinction should be marked between the political and geographical Tibet and the cultural area of Tibet. Political area has three parts in it: (i) U Tsang, (ii) Kham, and (iii) Amdo.

The political Tibet means the areas that were more or less directly controlled by the Tibetan governments of Lhasa before the Chinese invasion of 1949-50. However, the Tibet cultural areas encompassed the areas that are strongly influenced by Tibetan culture and religions. Countries on the south side of Himālayan division such as Bhutan, Sikkim in India, Mongolia, and areas of Chinese Turkistan, Central Asian countries bordering on political Tibet and some areas of present Russia.

Research Problems

Scholars seeking to write about Tibetan history, culture and literature face many difficulties. As Giuseppe Tucci wrote, "True historical facts are reduced to minimum" and further he concluded that, "We must discover them; almost guess them, here and there; hidden in wilderness of pious tales."[1] Since Buddhism came to influence almost all areas of Tibetan lives, and also because the history of their country is closely connected with Buddhism in the mind of Tibetans, traditional sources tend to overlay historical events with Buddhist significance and began to visualize the presence of Buddhist deities in important events. This process is so insidious in historical works that even the pre-Buddhist history of Tibet has been cast as a history of preparation of the country for dissemination of Buddhism. Not only this, even the pre-Buddhist faith Bon (believed to be founded by Shen Rab Mi Bo) has been unable to sustain itself independently and became a part of Buddhism, though with some ideological differences. However, Buddhism heavily shadows the Bon monasteries, their scriptures, method of worship and penances. And Buddhism of Tibet (and not Buddhism in General) has covered Bon with its wide acceptance. Tibetan historical records were composed by the people who saw their country's history as a record of gradual triumph of Buddhist religion over the indigenous forces opposing it. Their accounts presuppose a mythical structure in which forces of darkness and ignorance are defeated by the forces of *dharma*, and so the modern scholar who attempts to find historical truths in these is destined to meet with a great deal of frustration. The same happens when we try to find history of India from the great books of Vedic, Buddhism and Jainism where religion overlay the historical facts.

1. Tucci, p. 155.

However, fortunately, despite their deficiencies in history, Tibetan historical records expounds a great deal about how Tibetans have traditionally viewed themselves, their religion and their country. A bright ray of hope appears, when we tackle philosophical and literary works in Buddhism that are supposed to be the mirror of not only ideas, but the instances also and similes given in those books reflect their historical and social aspects.

Origin of the Race

Western science places the Tibetan race among the Mongolian family of nations which with their allied Turkish tribes inhabited high Asia from time immemorial. It is generally believed that the Tibetan came partly from the north-east and later from Assam and Burma in the south-east. Philologically the Tibetans belong to the same linguistic family as the Burmese. As far as the appearance goes, even now it is difficult to distinguish a Tibetan from Mongol, until he or she speaks. The early Tibetan would appear to have had an entirely pastoral life. It is among the shepherds and Yak-herdsmen that one can still find the purest type of race.

Tibet did not escape from the notice of the father of the history. Writing some 2400 years ago, Herodotus tells us of a rumour about a race of enormous ants that delved for gold in a country to the north-west of India. Perhaps the simple art is relating to Tibetan workmen with yak hair blanket to dig the gold mines in Thok Jalung in western Tibetan, which is cold, and windy area.[2]

According to traditional Tibetan sources, Tibetan race is descendent from the union of a Monkey and an Ogress. The Monkey was an incarnation of Avalokiteśvara (སྤྱན་རས་གཟིགས།), the Buddha of compassion, and the Ogress was strong willed, driven by sexual forces, an animal. From their union, six offspring were born who were without tails and walked upright. Therefore, it is generally believed that the nature of

2. Herodotus, Book III, Chapter, 102-105.

Tibetan race can be traced back to the resultant nature of these two progenitors. Their gentleness and compassion are traced back to the Monkey, but their wilfulness, avarice, etc., traits are derived from the Ogress.[3]

After planting the seeds of Tibetan race, Avalokiteśvara (སྤྱན་རས་གཟིགས།) continued to take an interest in the spiritual development of the country because the early Tibetans were too primitive to be able to understand or adopt Buddhism. However, he decided to work behind the scene to help them reach a level of maturity that would allow them to become Buddhist. Since the incarnation of Avalokiteśvara (སྤྱན་རས་གཟིགས།) was the progenitor of Tibetan race, the importance of Avalokiteśvara can be understood in the light of above given facts.

Early Kings of Tibet

The first king of Tibet, as popular origin myth contents, was from India and he was the son of an Indian king Śatāyuddha (དམག་བརྒྱ། in Tibetan).[4] According to Red Annals, a king from the clan of Kurus, who fled from India to Tibet fearing the act of reprisal, he was named Nya Thi Tsan Po meaning Neck-throne king and built his house near Tsang Po River in the Yarlung valley, was the first king of Tibet. (Tsang Po flows from Tibet to India under name Brahmaputra.)

The early kings of Tibet were described as adherents of Bon. Bon was concoction of Shamanism and animistic practices. In sixth century AD, when the emergent empire of Tibet began to expand outward, it discovered that it was surrounded on all side by Buddhist civilizations. Till that time Buddhism had grown up and established its firm feet in the Gangetic plain and one of the major contributors of it was the great Indian Emperor Aśoka. In third century BC and in intervening centuries, a number of monastic universities have been built

3. Wangyal, p. 59.
4. Tulku, p. IX.

in northern part of India until the sixth century AD at the time of introduction of Buddhism in Tibet. Buddhism had also established itself in Gilgit, Baltistan and had penetrated into Central Asia and beyond, following ancient trade routes. Buddhist missionaries travelled the world atop Pāmīr's mountains, bringing Buddhism to China through the caravan routes that passed to the north and south of the Taklamakan desert. Through the southern routes, it passed through the kingdoms of Shan and Khoṭan. Both of which were Buddhist countries, and the northern route went through the cities of Karashahr, Kuccha and Kashgar, all of which were under Chinese control. To the south of Tibet was the kingdom of Nepal, which at that time encompassed little more than the Kāṭhmāṇḍu valley. It was strongly influenced by Indian culture and had a number of Buddhist monasteries and temples.[5]

Early Tibet and China

In the early part of sixth century AD, Tibetan army conquered and annexed large area of Central Asia that lay between Tibet and China and were inhabited by nomadic and semi-nomadic tribes of Turkic and Tibetan stock. In AD 635 Tibet attacked China itself and in successive campaigns managed to wrest control of large area that had been under Chinese control. These included four main Chinese strongholds in Chinese Turkistan.

The first appearance of Buddhism in Tibet seem to have occurred during the reign of King Lha Tho-Tho-Ri-Nyentsen (born AD 173), who was 23rd king from Nya Thi Tsen Po.[6]

According to Tibetan legends, one day a Buddhist text and relics consecrated to Avalokiteśvara (སྤྱན་རས་གཟིགས།) fell from the sky on the roof of King's palace. That book was

5. Richardson, p. 26-27.

6. 1. Nya Rhi Tsan Po the name of 32 kings prior to Song Tsan Gampo

Karaṇḍavyūha Sūtra[7] (ཟ་མ་ཏོག་བཀོད་པའི་མདོ།). Tsepon Shakabpa cites a Tibetan account that indicates that these articles (book and relics) were actually brought from India, but King Lha Tho-Tho-Ri Nyentsen hid their origin. After having a dream indicating that in four generations,[8] a king will be able to read and understand this book. That prophecy regarding the reading of the book proved true when the great king Songsen Gampo became the 33rd king of Tibet and also became instrumental in spreading the *dharma* of Buddha from India. The arrival of this text may be considered the first introduction of Buddhism in Tibet, and is believed to have been planned. This event has got so much importance in Tibet that their currency before the Chinese takeover was dated in terms of years in which this event took place, held by Tibetan historians to be in the year AD 233.[9]

The Religious Kings of Tibet and the Period of First Dissemination of Buddhism (སྔ་དར)

The first transmission of Buddhism into Tibet occurred during the reign of 33rd king of Tibet (as according to the prediction of the book earlier), Srong Tsen Gampo (སྲོང་བཙན་སྒམ་པོ།). He was the first among the three religious kings and famous among the Tibetan scholars as ཆོས་རྒྱལ་གསུམ།. He is considered to be an incarnation of Avalokiteśvara, who took rebirth as a king in order to further the dissemination of *dharma*. Under his military guidance, Tibet became a major power in Central Asia, and when it spread beyond its original borders it encountered Buddhism, which was widespread in Central Asia and China. During his reign, Tibet conquered the kingdom of Shangshung (now western Tibet) and he moved his capital from Yarlung to Lhasa. At that time, it was known as Rasa,

7. Thanka, p. 23.
8. According to some other traditional sources, the number of generation indicated was another way and it was indicated that after 32nd king there will be a king who will be able to make this book readable and be instrumental to decipher its meaning.
9. Shakabpa, pp. 24-25.

meaning enclosure, suggesting that the area was originally a hunting preserve with a royal residence on the top of the Marpori hill. A palace was built on the hill[10] and Rasa became Lhasa (ལྷ་ས) meaning, "The land of God." The nomenclature was done considering the religious nature of country and the impact of Buddhism upon it. The name itself shows the royal patronage and the people's support to Buddhism in such intense form that the whole capital was named as Lhasa (Lha in Tibetan means God and Sa is Tibetan for land). Until date, this name remained unchanged. Though after Chinese occupation, the tradition of changing the name of all places into Chinese language is taking place.

Seeking political alliance, Srong Tsen Gam Po sent emissaries to King Ansuvarman and Tai-Tsung, the king of Nepal and King Tang dynasty of China respectively. The king of Nepal, Ansuvarman pleasantly agreed to do so, and his daughter Bhr̥kuṭi married to the king of Tibet. But the king of Tang dynasty in China did not agreed willingly but after defeat in battle with Srong Tsen Gam Po, he had to give his daughter Wen-Cheng to the Tibetan king.

Both the marriages were very fruitful in Tibet with respect to Buddhism and in fact both Nepalese and Chinese princes, to some extent proved to be instrumental in introducing Buddhism in the royal palace of Tibet. Both princesses were Buddhist by faith and they brought with themselves statues of Buddha. The Nepalese princess brought with her Buddha Amitābha (མི་ཁྲུགས་པ།). It was ensconced in a temple she had built in the centre of a lake Ramoche. Nepalese princes referred to by Tibetan as Belsa and Trisum, meaning Nepalese wife and royal lady. The Chinese princess Wen Chang brought with her the image of Śākyamuni (ས་སྐྱ་ཐུབ་པ།) it was installed in a temple named Trulnag nowadays known as Jokhang. It is considered as the holiest shrines of Tibet and its circumambulation is considered pious and, it is also customary

10. Now the site of Poṭala; Traditional Residence of Dalai Lamas up to 1959.

for every Tibetan visitor. Due to Chinese princess, the Chinese culture gained a strong influence in royal court of Tibet. Later on, both the princesses were taken by Tibetan as Tārā, the suitable match for Avalokiteśvara (སྤྱན་རས་གཟིགས།).

Literary Contacts

The period of Srong Tsen Gam Po is characterized by a growing perception on the part of ruling class that Tibet lagged behind many of its neighbours culturally and many perceived Buddhism as an integral part of these advanced foreign cultures.

One of the most obvious gaps in the Tibetan culture until that was lack of literary script or a common grammar. To introduce Buddhism and to make a language with grammar, King Srong Tsen Gampo sent his minister Thonmi Sambhota (son of Thonmi Anu) with sixteen companions to India on the mission to study in order to prepare the task of introducing a grammar and suitable literary script and also to study Buddhism. Thonmi reached Nālandā in AD 632[11], which at that time was the biggest residential university in Asia and famous all over the world (Nālandā Mahāvihāra). He studied there and learned Sanskrit with other branches of study. He learned Sanskrit language from Lipikāra Brāhmaṇa. He studied Pāṇini, Kalapa and Candra (grammar part), Political Science, 21 *sūtras* of Avalokiteśvara (སྤྱན་རས་གཟིགས།) and Tantra from Puṇḍit Deva Vidyā Singh. Thonmi Sambhota returned Tibet with the great treasure of Indian books of Buddhism.

Thonmi remained in India for a number of years and when he reached Tibet, all of his companions died during this journey due to climatic diversities from Tibet and also within India. Only Thonmi managed to return and was able to fulfil his task of creating a grammar and script for Tibetan language. It may also be possible that Thonmi managed to sustain at the cost of his companions. However, he returned to Tibet

---

11. Samten Norbu, "A Short history of Tibetan Translated Literature," *Tibet Journal*, vol. 1.

and let the king know his accomplishments. Then the great work of creating the script for the dialects of Tibetan language started.

UCHEN AND UMED SCRIPT (ཡི་གེ་དབུ་ཅན་དང་དབུ་མེད།)

The origins of Tibetan script are undoubtedly a matter of great controversy. The renowned twentieth-century scholar monk and the writer of Tibbati Pathmala Tulku Dondub, is of the opinion that the script today of Tibetan language, which is built by Thonmi, has been taken from the Sanskrit language in Devanāgarī script. Some other scholars have suggested that it is based on the Rajñnā script of the Gupta period. In my opinion the Tibetan Uchen script has been inspired from the Devanāgarī script only and there is a reason behind it. Because the principal aim of Thonmi was to introduce Buddhist scripture into Tibet, he was bound to take the alphabet of the language in which the Buddhist texts were written. Furthermore, the book that was found on the top of the king's palace centuries ago was in Sanskrit. Therefore, the task of Thonmi was not simple but a complex one. He had to invent a script that carried both the properties of Sanskrit and Tibetan.

Therefore, in order to fulfil his task, Thonmi took the alphabet of Sanskrit, eliminated 12 consonants and add 6 from Tibetan in it. Then he took the vowels and selected only four vowels. Following are the consonants and vowels of Tibetan alphabet:

There are thirty consonants. They called Saljed Sumcu (གསལ་བྱེད་གསུམ་བཅུ།) in Tibetan. In addition, there are only four vowels contrary to 16 in Sanskrit. They are called yang Zhi (དབྱངས་བཞི།).

༄༅། །གསལ་བྱེད་གསུམ་བཅུ།

ཀ་ ཁ་ ག་ ང་། ཅ་ ཆ་ ཇ་ ཉ།

ཏ་ ཐ་ ད་ ན། པ་ ཕ་ བ་ མ།

ཙ་ཚ་ཛ་ཝ། ཞ་ཟ་འ་ཡ།

ར་ལ་ཤ་ས་ཧ་ཨ།།

དབྱངས་བཞི།

ཨི། ཨུ། ཨེ། ཨོ།

But the Sanskrit treatises which were to be translated and transliterated need more sounds than the thirty Tibetan consonants cover. Furthermore, some Sanskrit words (Mantra and Tāntric words, etc.) cannot be translated and therefore, there was need to transcribe them fully. Hence Thonmi created Tibetan equivalents for all the Sanskrit syllables. Following is the Tibetan equivalent alphabet of Sanskrit consonants and vowels:

ཨ་ ཨཱ་ ཨི་ ཨཱི་ ཨུ་ ཨཱུ་ རྀ་ རཱྀ་ ལྀ་ ལཱྀ་

ཨེ་ ཨཻ་ ཨོ་ ཨཽ་ ཨཾ་ ཨཿ།

ཀ་ ཁ་ ག་ གྷ་ ང་།

ཙ་ ཚ་ ཛ་ ཛྷ་ ཉ།

ཏ་ ཐ་ ད་ དྷ་ ན།

པ་ ཕ་ བ་ བྷ་ མ།

ཡ་ ར་ ལ་ ཝ་ ཤ་ ས་ ཥ་ ཧ།

ཀྵ ཕ ཧྱ།

The Tibetan equivalents for some sanskrit equivalents are called the six reversed letters. They are the following:

ཊ་ ཋ་ ཌ་ ཥ་ ཎ་ ཀྵ་

Thus the task of creating script for Tibetan language has been completed. He had chosen only six syllables from the

Tibetan dialects. Rest 24 main consonants and four vowels were from the then court language of Indian kings, i.e., Sanskrit. These six consonants were:

ཙ་ ཚ་ ཛ་ ཞ་ ཟ་ and འ།

But while making the grammar, Thonmi did not take the base of Sanskrit language. He did it in his own native language and script. So, this is the very reason that Tibetan script, though based and inspired from Sanskrit language, has pronunciation and writing method is quite different and suitabily close to Tibetans and not to Sanskrit-speaking people. This was done knowingly to suit the Tibetan masses. However, after completion of the grammar development, the king used his authority to declare that the system developed by Thonmi Sambhota would henceforth be standard throughout the area ruled by the Central government. Prior to this, king himself learned Buddhism and the new grammer of Tibetan language from Thonmi.

Then Thonmi translated various books of *Sūtra Piṭaka* and others including 21 *sūtra*s of Avalokiteśvara (སྤྱན་རས་གཟིགས།)

So, the formal introduction of Buddhism in Tibet was done, but to make Buddhism functional, the actual work of establishing the Buddhist practices was yet to be done. The establishment of Budhist monasteries, the ordination of Tibetan into monkhood are the major works among other which remained to be done.

First Dissemination of Buddhism or Nga Dar (སྔ་དར།)

This work was handled by next great king of Tibet named Thi Srong Detsen (ཁྲི་སྲོང་ལྡེའུ་བཙན།) (*circa* AD 740-98). He was considered by Tibetan to have been an incarnation of Buddha of wisdom, Mañjuśrī. By all account, he was a devout Buddhist who took personal interest in the propagation of Buddhism. In order to accomplish this, he sent a message to the great Indian scholar Śāntarakṣita (ཞི་བ་འཚོ།) asking him to come to Tibet further carry out the establishment work of

Buddhism which was fragmentary at that time. Śāntarakṣita was Abbot of Vikramaśilā monastery, which was one of the greatest Tāntric seat of learning in India (Vikramaśilā is near Bhāgalpur in Bihar in the vicinity of Mandāra hill, the abode of Lord Śiva). Śāntarakṣita called Byang Chub Kyi Khyen Po (བྱང་ཆུབ་ཀྱི་མཁན་པོ།) in Tibet.

When Śāntarakṣita arrived in Tibet for the full-fledged introduction of Buddhism in Tibet, he was confronted by many local forces. The practitioners of Bon and other local Shamanist faith feared alienation of their traditional values and system. Many of them were ministers in the court of Thi Srong Detsen (ཁྲི་སྲོང་ལྡེའུ་བཙན།). So, Śāntarakṣita didn't get proper support from royal and aristocrat families. Unfortunately, there were several natural calamities in Tibet during that period and it was taken as the signs of wrathfulness of Bon deities. Thus, Śāntarakṣita could not accomplish his work and it was interpreted that the arrival of new faith caused the wrath in local religion or faith. So, Śāntarakṣita was forced to leave Tibet but before leaving, he advised the king to invite Padmasambhava (པདམ་འབྱུང་ནས).

According to traditional history, Padmasambhava knew in advance by his *yogic* power that the king of Tibet would invite him in order to fulfil the task of introducing Buddhism in Tibet. So, when the messenger arrived with the messege of king Thi Srong Detsen (ཁྲི་སྲོང་ལྡེའུ་བཙན།) to come Tibet, he was already prepared to leave his place and fight with all Shamanist demon and deities of Tibet. When he entered the outer reaches of Tibet, the demonic forces saught to bar his progress by sending a huge snowstorm as expected. But Padmasambhava retreated to cave and entered into a deep meditation and through this, he was able to defeat the demonistic purposes. As he travelled towards central Tibet, the demons and deities of the country confronted him but Padmasambhava had great Tāntric and magical powers and by that he single-handedly defeated them all. The people of Tibet were amazed that a single man could challenge their powerful demons to personal combat and triumph.

Because of this victory, Padmasambhava, popularly known through Tibet as པདམ་འབྱུང་ནས, was able to overcome human opposition, after which he advised the king to invite Śāntarakṣita again. In AD 775, the Tibetan King Thi Srong Detsen (ཁྲི་སྲོང་ལྡེ་བཙན) invited Śāntarakṣita and they together founded the first monastery of Tibet "Sam Ye" བསམ་ཡས. The monastery was built in *maṇḍala* pattern, with a temple in the centre and its four sides oriented with cardinal directions. It was said to have been modelled after the great monastery of Odantapurī in Bihar.[12] The monastery was completed in AD 766 and consecrated in AD 767.[13] "Sam Ye can be regarded as the symbol of the sun from which the rays of *dharma* spread all over Tibet in the course of time."[14] When the monastery was finished, seven Tibetan received monastic vows (སྡོམ་པ་ཕོག་བྱིན་པ།). They later came to be known as, "seven probationers" and their ordination is considered to be the inauguration of monastic Buddhism in Tibet.

After this, king embarked upon the work of the translation of Buddhist scriptures that were brought by Thonmi Sambhota, realizing that Buddhism can only be establish and accepted in the Tibetan hearts when it is in the language of the land. He invited translators from India and even China. He also sent young Tibetan to India for the training in Buddhism and its language.

The Two Paths of Enlightenment

During this time, Buddhism had already started flourishing. Nevertheless, the local beliefs of Tibetan people gathered under the leadership of a person named Hashang, who undertook a scholarly debate with the Indian scholar Kamalaśīla engrossed in the work of propagation of Buddhism in Tibet. The debate was in fact organized by the king of Tibet himself to expound the clarity of Buddhism

12. G Tucci, 1956, pp. 279-81.
13. Haarh, pp. 121-70.
14. Bhutia, p. 135.

from the Indian and Hashang perspective. Actually, Hashang represented the Mahāyāna School of Buddhism in China, which was centrally focused on concentration of *dhyāna*. The debate was very fruitful and the Tibetan Buddhist believes that the debate ended with a clear victory of Indian gradualist school of Buddhism and the defeat of Chinese teaching of sudden enlightenment. Sources agree that the Chinese teachings of sudden enlightenment were popular in Tibet, but after the debate or council as some call it, subsequently declined. The widespread disapproval of such doctrine at that time, shadow today's practitioners also and among contemporary Tibetan scholars it may be observed that the school which speaks of sudden enlightenment, often feels compelled to argue that their teachings are significantly distinct from those of Hashang Mahāyāna and are from the Tantric school of Vajrayāna. Whether this story is having some truth in it or not, this may be questioned. However, the presence of this story until date among Tibetan folklore shows that historically somewhere there was a conflict between Indian gradual school and Chinese sudden enlightenment school and the Indian model eventually won out. Here I am forced to point out one important change in the acceptance of the Buddhist practices in Tibetan Buddhism that is acceptable to Tibetans. It is said that Hashang, with his followers committed suicide after his defeat by Kamalaśīla and Gyānendra. After long passage of time, the emergence of Vajrayāna took place in Tibetan Buddhism and we know that Vajrayāna advocates for the enlightenment in one life time which in turn means the path of sudden enlightenment. Now in present time, both the gradual and sudden enlightenment paths to *nirvāṇa* are present in the Tibetan Buddhism and are accepted. They do not cross one another. Rather my teacher, who happens to be a Lama and was, teaching in Sera monastery in Tibet during the Chinese invasion, opines that both the paths support one another and they deal with different status of the practitioner.

The third great religious king who made Buddhism more popular was Ralpachan (815-838 AD). King Ralpachan was said to have been an emanation of Buddha Vajrapāṇi (རྡོ་རྗེ་འཆང་།)

The Translations

One of the major contributions of his reign was his sponsorship of a project to standardize translations equivalent for Buddhist texts. The project headed by Beltsek created a glossary for Sanskrit and Tibetan terms and revised the written language so that Tibetan translation could more accurately reflect the grammar and syntax of Sanskrit. By this time, there were a number of highly trained Tibetan translators (ལོ་ཙཱ་བ) such as Yeshe De, and many more scholars at home. Committees made up of Indian and Tibetan scholars translated most text; the Indian were mainly responsible for ratifying the doctrinal accuracy of the translation, while the Tibetans made it sure that they were grammatically correct. Since both the Tibetans and Indians were generally well-versed in Buddhist thought and practice, so there was also considerable overlap in translation duties. The translation produced during this period continue to be favoured by the Nyingmā school of Tibetan Buddhism, which considers them to be more faithful to the original spirit of the text than the later translations prepared during the period of second dissemination of Buddhism after the King Lang Dharma's destruction. The king Ralpachan (ཁྲི་རལ་པ་ཅན) is said to have been an emanation of Vajrapāṇi. By all accounts, he was deeply committed to Buddhism, his fervour led him to concentrate on religious matter, and to neglect the affairs of the state. He spent lavish amount of money on the construction of temples and monasteries and supported visits by Indian scholars as well as trips to India by Tibetan scholars. He is reported to have been so devoted to *dharma* that in official state ceremonies, he would tie ribbons to his long braids, and Buddhist monks would sit on top of the braids, symbolizing the submission to the *saṅgha*.[15] He started a policy which according to a group of seven household had to support each monk, which means that even those who had little or no interest in Buddhism were required to finance its propagation. The reaction against Ralpachan's mishandling of the government was eventually so intense that he was assassinated by two of his ministers, who crept up behind him and twisted his neck while he was relaxing in his palace. Although traditional sources portray the growing opposition to his reign was an underhanded plotting by adherents of Bon. Eventually it seems that his political ineptitude and financial irresponsi-bilities were the root cause of his eventual downfall.

Lang Dharma

King Ralpachan was succeeded by Lang Dharma (reign 838-42), who is reported to have vigorously persecuted Buddhism. The persecution brought an end to the period of the first dissemination of Buddhism, which was initiated by the religious kings of the seventh century.

Traditional sources portray Lang Dharma as a devout adherent of Bon, who was possessed by a demon. W.D. Shakabpa wrote in his book that "After Lang Dharma's death rumours circulated that he had horns on his head and a black tongue."[16] Shakabpa also states that, "the Tibetan custom of greeting people by stretching one's head and sticking out one's tongue originally led a way of indicating that — unlike Lang Dharma they lacked horns and black tongue."[17]

Here one thing is noteworthy. The spread of Buddhism in Tibet was primarily in terms of royal patronage, but even during the period of persecution, Buddhism continued to spread throughout the country. While the construction of temples and monasteries may have been halted, Buddhist

15. Franke, chapter II, Nyingma.
16. Shakabpa, p. 53.
17. *Ibid.*, pp. 53-55.

teachers apparently continued to circulate the religion, and followers of Bon were incorporating Buddhist ideas and practices into their own tradition. With the result, it eventually became essentially a divergent school of Buddhism.

So, during Lang Dharma's period, the temples and monasteries were shut down, monks and nuns were forced to return tc lay life. Cultural contacts with India were halted and many religious leader of Tibet migrated beyond the king's sphere of influences, i.e., in Central Asian regions. Traditional sources say that in western Tibet, Buddhism remained in a strong position even during Lang Dharma's period. Lang Dharma was also killed by a monk named Belgyi Dorje during a theatrical performance. Lang Dharma's death led to the collapse of the Yarlung dynasty and brought on a period of political chaos in Tibet. It marks the end of Tibetan empire in Central Asia. With no strong authority in Tibet to hold the empire together, China was able to regain control over the areas it had lost and Tibetans receded behind their older mountain. It was until AD 1247 that another strong central authority was established in Tibet, when Śākya Puṇḍit was appointed overlord of Tibet by the Mongol chieftain Godan, a grandson of Ghengis Khan.

The Revival or the Second Dissemination of Buddhism or Phyi Dar (ཕྱི་དར།)

Near the end of tenth century, according to traditional accounts, Tsenpo Khore, the king of western province of Guge, renounced the throne and became a Buddhist monk, taking the ordination name Yeshe Od (ཡེ་ཤེས་འོད). Apparently, intending to revive *dharma* in Tibet, he sent 21 promising Tibetan monks to India to study, and he allocated money to support Buddhist scholarship in Tibet. All but two monks died in India, but the two who returned became prominent scholars and translators.[18] They were Rin Chen Zang Po རིན་ཆེན་བཟང་པོ

18. The Tibetan term for translator is Lotsa Ba and for scholars is Panchen (literally means great *puṇḍit*).

and Lekbe Sherab, who returned to Tibet in 978, along with some Indian scholars. This event is thought to mark the inauguration of second dissemination ཕྱི་དར of Buddhism in Tibet. The greatest Tibetan figure of this period was Rin Chen Zang Po (རིན་ཆེན་བཟང་པོ) who oversaw the translation of many Sanskrit *sūtra*s and Tantras, along with their voluminous commentaries. He made three visits to India, spent total 17 years there, travelling from teacher to teacher, receiving initiations and oral instructions, acquiring copies of Buddhist texts. He brought them back with him to Tibet, and his literary activity played a significant role in the Buddhist renaissance ཕྱི་དར།.[19,20]

Atīśa

The most important event of this period, however, was arrival of the Indian scholar Atīśa in Tibet [Full name Atīśa Dīpaṅkar Śrījñāna AD 982-1054 (ཨ་ཏི་ཤ་མར་མེ་མཛད་དཔལ་འབྱུང་། is also one of the fame of Atīśa in Tibetan)] which according to traditional sources occurred in AD 1042. At his arrival in Guge, Atīśa was 60.

According to David Snellgrove and Hugh Richardson,

> Atisha's authority and prestige gave a new direction to the thinking and practice of other religious teachers in Tibet, and he certainly attracted the attention of ordinary people to such an extent that the dominance of Buddhism over the whole range of Tibetan social life was never thereafter seriously challenged.

Atīśa's composition of *The Lamp for the Path to Enlightenment* (བྱང་ཆུབ་ལམ་གྱི་སྒྲོན་མ)[21] is among many literary works, which Tibet got. Atīśa was of the view that there is not any discrepancy between Mahāyāna and Tantra.[22] Atīśa died in Tibet in AD

19. Giuseppe Rinchen.
20. Negi, 1994.
21. Restored in Sanskrit and other language by Central Institute of Higher Tibetan Studies, Sarnath, Varanasi.
22. Powers.

1054. Atīśa's instruction and influence led to the founding of bKa Dam Pa (བཀའ་དམས་པ།) sect of Buddhism in Tibet. In 1054 Dromtonpa founded Reting monastery, which became main seat of learning of བཀའ་དམས་པ in Tibet.

Indigenous Schools and Śākya Puṇḍit

During the centuries after Atīśa's death, Buddhism continued to flourish in Tibet. As Tibetans became more confident in their grasp of the tradition, indigenous schools began to develop. The first of this kind was from Śākya (ས་སྐྱ།) sect, although the branch of Buddhism which was established by Padmasambhava was there and it was named in Tibetan as (རྙིང་མ།) but it cannot be called indigenous because it was established with the help of Indian scholars including Padmasambhava. Śākya took its name from the monastery of Śākya founded by Kun Chog Gyalpo [དཀོན་མཆོག་རྒྱལ་པོ། (1034-1102)] of Khon family in 1073. His son and descendant Ānandagarbha (ཀུན་དགའ་སྙིང་པོ།) (1092-1158) systematized the teachings of the lineage, which is traced to Drokmi, who travelled to India and brought back Tāntric and scholastic teachings. (ཀུན་དགའ་སྙིང་པོ) or Ānandagarbha also became famous as the "Great Sakya pa."

Early in twelfth century, Mongols emerged as the new power in Central Asia under the rule and leadership of Ghengis Khan. In AD 1240, the Mongol chieftain Godan invaded Tibet raiding and looting almost as far as Lhasa. In 1249, Godan summoned Kun Ga Gyaltsan Pal Sangpo (ཀུན་དགའ་རྒྱལ་མཚན་དཔལ་བཟང་པོ) better known as Śākya Puṇḍit, the most eminent religious leader of his day, to surrender his country to Mongol control. When Śākya Puṇḍit met the Khan, however, the Mongol ruler was so much impressed with him that he became converted to Buddhism. He promised to protect Tibet against foreign threats and Śākya Lama would become spiritual preceptors of the Mongol Khans. It was patron-priest relationship "Yon-Chog" (ཡོན་མཆོག).

In 1251, both Śākya Puṇḍit and Godan died but the patron priest relationship continued by Kublai Khan. Actually, under Mongol supremacy the Tibetan Śākyas ruled independently. It was an age of political intrigues, and many religious leaders of various sects such as Karma Pa, Tsel Pa, and GriGung Pa were engaged in factionalism. They were jealous by the rapid ascent to power of Pakpa (Śākya Puṇḍit's nephew) who also enjoyed Mongol patronage. Many of the large monasteries created their own armies of warrior monks. After Kublai until Timor, the Mongol patronage was continued to Śākyas.

Tibetan Piṭakas (སྡེ་སྣོད་གསུམ)

Although this was a period of conflict between different head of the sects, this period witnessed the compilation of the Tibetan canons in two sections *Kanjur* (collection of trans-lation of the Buddha's teachings) and *Tanjur* (collection of the translation of Buddhist treatises and indigenous Tibetan books on Buddhism). The *Kanjur* contains the words and teachings of Buddha's whereas *Tanjur* contains voluminous commentarial literature that had came to Tibet from India as well as some indigenous Tibetan works (detailed contents are already given in this Chapter). The great scholar Bu Ton was primarily associated with this project.[23]

When the compilation of Tibetan canon was completed, wood blocks were carved for the entire collection, a process that required a vast amount of effort, both in the carving and in proofreading. In this traditional Tibetan printing technique, a mirror image of the page is carefully carved in leaf. The block is then inked and the paper pressed against the inked surface. The initial carving requires a great deal of time, but when it is completed, numerous copies can be produced. The manuscript copies were kept at the monastery of Narthang.

23. Ruegg, 1966.

A key figure in the eventual demise of Śākya power was བྱང་ཆུབ་རྒྱལ་མཚན། (AD 1302-64), who belongs to the Lang family. He tried his best to eradicate all traces of Mongol influence and hearkening back to the glories of the dynasty of religious kings (ཆོས་རྒྱལ།). After 130 years of his death the prince of Rinbug, who had been a minister of earlier kings ascended to throne. Then Tsang rulers came, who by AD 1565 had consolidated their power.

The Gelugs

During the fifteenth century, the successors of Bodhi Dhvaja (བྱང་ཆུབ་རྒྱལ་མཚན།) ruled Tibet, TsongkhaPa (1357-1419), one of the greatest ever scholar Tibet has produced, founded a new school of Tibetan Buddhism, which has come to be known as Gelug Pa (དགེ་ལུགས་པ།) meaning, "System of virtue." TsongkhaPa himself had little interest in politics, and his early successors followed his examples. As time went on, however, their influence grew, with the result that they eventually came out on top of the power hierarchy. Now the present Dalai Lama, Tenzin Gyatso too, belongs to this sect and hence instrumental in propagation of the Gelug ideas also.

At first, the new order (Gelug) won the respect of older schools, mostly because of its strict observance of monastic discipline, its strong emphasis on study and meditation, and its disinterest in political involvements. However, during the time of Gendun Gyatso, one of the rulers of Tibet later declared second Dalai Lama, this new school with its high standards of disciplines and scholarship began to attract the active resentment of some of the older orders, which often suffered in comparison. Gendun Gyatso's growing prestige and high regard in which his school was held caused KarmaPa hierarchs and other lay patron to move against him, with the result that for most of his life he was not able to live in GelugPa monasteries around Lhasa. Because of this, he travelled widely throughout the country, and his personal sanctity and good reputation won many converts. He was an effective missionary and spokesman for TsongkhaPa's lineage, and his personal sanctity for adherence to monastic discipline, scholarship and meditative attainments, helped him to gain large number of disciples and admirers.

Dalai Lamas

Gendun Gyatso was succeeded by Sonam Gyatso (1543-88). He continued the missionary works of his predecessors, that time he visited the Altan Khan, the chief of Tumid Mongols. When the Lama and khan met, the latter conferred the title of Tali (literally meaning Ocean) on Sonam Gyatso, implying that he was an Ocean of wisdom. Thus, he and his successors (and retrospectively two predecessors) came to be known as Tali and later on Dalai Lama.

Because of Sonam Gyatso's influence, many Mongols gave up Bon sacrifices and converted to Buddhism (Gelug sect). After Sonam Gyatso, his reincarnation was discovered in the person of a great grandson of Altan Khan, who received the ordination of Yon Tan Gyatso (ཡོན་ཏན་རྒྱ་མཚོ) (fourth Dalai Lama). The confrontation between Gelugs and Karmas were further strained. Yon tan Gyatso died in 1617 and it was widely rumoured that he was poisoned.

The successor of fourth Dalai Lama, fifth Dalai Lama, Ngawang Losang Gyatso (1617-82) popularly referred to as the Great Fifth was the most dynamic and influential of the early Dalai Lamas. He was a great leader, and accomplished Tāntric *yogī*, and an exceptional writer. His literary output surpasses the combined total of all the other Dalai Lamas. He united the three provinces of Tibet and with the help of his Mongol benefactors; he became the first Dalai Lama to rule a unified Tibet in AD 1642.

Despite the power of his allies, it took some time for the Dalai Lama to extend his power over all of Tibet, but in AD 1656, he controlled an area that extended over the region of Mount Kailash in the west to Kham province of Tibet in East.[24]

24. Powers.

Although he was heavy handed with Jonang Pas and Karma Pas, his treatment of other order was often generous. He was particularly supportive of Nyingma (རྙིང་མ), and he himself was an ardent practitioner of several Nyingma Tantric lineages.

Later Dalai Lamas

During the seventeenth and eighteenth century, Tibet became increasingly isolated from its neighbours. When it first adopted Buddhism, it was surrounded by Buddhist civilizations; but by this time, it was the only country in the region in which Buddhism was predominant. Despite a growing conviction that Tibet was the only country in which the true *dharma* flourished, outside influences were still generally welcomed. There were communities of Muslims in Tibet, where members often performed tasks like butchering animals that were repugnant to Tibetan Buddhist sensibilities. Many Newaries from Nepal, whose religion was a mix of Hindu and Buddhist elements, were valued craftsmen famous for their superb religious artworks. In seventeenth century, Christian missionaries also visited Tibet. However, they could not convince more than a handful of Tibetans to convert.

After the death (or murdered by Mongols?) of sixth Dalai Lama Tsayang Gyatso, Kelsang Gyatso became next Dalai Lama. However, the VIIth Dalai could enthrone only in 1720. Kelsang Gyatso was an exemplary monk who lived a simple life in accordance with the rules of monastic discipline. He also wrote important works on several Tāntric sets including Heruka Cakrasaṁvara, Vajrabhairava, Kālacakra and Guhyasamāja. He died in 1757 at the age of 50. After the death of VIIth Dalai lama, the period of 130 years began where none of the Dalai Lamas assumed effective control. During this time, the country was ruled by a succession of regents, all of whom were GelugPa monks. Even during VIIIth Dalai, Jamphel Gyatso, regents handled the administration. The next four Dalai Lama died young. By and large, the regents managed to maintain stability.

Thirteenth Dalai Lama

In 1875, Thinley Gyatso became XIIth Dalai Lama. His successor Thubten Gyatso [ཐུབ་བསྟན་རྒྱ་མཚོ་ (1876-1933)] lived much longer and he became one of the greatest rulers in Tibetan History. He had great broad vision and he wanted his country to be compatible with the modern nations of the West. In his attempt to enlist foreign allies, the XIIIth Dalai Lama discovered that Tibet had no friend in the international community and utterly lacked the military resources to repel a determined foreign invasion. On its borders a new power was growing, one that would eventually engulf Tibet, and all of the Dalai Lama's efforts to forestall catastrophe ultimately came to nothing. In a famous statement shortly before his death, he warned his people of imminent danger from foreign invasion and predicted that unless Tibet adopted his modern policies the country would be overrun, its people killed or enslaved, and its religion destroyed.[25] After his death in 1933, the combination of Chinese manipulation of foreign powers and Tibetan insularity had isolated the country from the outside world. Despite his personal authority, however, after the death of XIIIth Dalai Lama, his reforms were mostly scuttled and Tibet returned to its policy of conservative isolation.[26]

In January 1934, Tenzin Gyatso, the present Dalai Lama was born and at the age of 13, he ascended the throne. Due to the Chinese occupation in the name of peaceful liberation, he along with his followers fled to India in 1959 and from then on he is residing in Dharamaśālā, Himachal Pradesh, a small township having climate similar to Lhasa.

---

25. John Avedon, *In Exile from the land of Snows* ; New York, Vintage Publications;1986, p. 3.

26. Powers, p. 161.

3

Padmasambhava and Nyingma School

(༄༅། །པདྨ་འབྱུང་གནས་དང་ཆོས་ལུགས་རྙིང་མ།)

Early Tibet

THE cultural heritage and civilization of Tibet can be traced back to three thousand years according to recorded sources and up to 10,000 years according to Bon Chronology. It means that the Tibetan civilization is one of the oldest in the world. It is no longer valid to assert that Tibetan script and culture did not exist before the advent of Buddhism in Tibet. Modern scholars have unequivocally accepted the existence of native culture before the emergence of Buddhism in Tibet, which is referred to as pre-Buddhist culture. In various historical records, we find references to the Zhang-Zhung script employed during this period. Therefore, we cannot but accept that this culture (pre-Buddhist culture known as Bon) provided the foundation of Tibetan literature and civilization, despite the fact that from seventh century onwards Tibet imported many aspects of Indian culture as Buddhism came to be adopted as the state religion and became popular religion under the native name later known as (རྙིང་མ) (Nyingma, literary it means old).

Contact with India

In fact, the contacts between Tibet and India began in second century AD during the reign of Lha-Tho-Tho-Ri gNyan-brTsan ལྷ་ཐོ་ཐོ་རི་གཉན་བཙན་། (AD 173-293), as marked by legend indicating the arrival of first three Buddhist texts. It was already stated in the introduction that how the mission of Thonmi Sambhota started during the reign of 33rd king Srong Tsen Gam Po and also how he succeeded to bring the Buddhist treatises and made the Tibetan script Uchan and Umed.

Śāntarakṣita and the First Attempt

After compilation of Tibetan grammar and scripts (Uchen and U-med), King Srong Tsen Gam Po wished to become Buddhist. He also wanted to declare Buddhism as a state religion in order to benefit all the people of his empire by the teachings of Buddha. To do so, the first task was to establish the Buddhist monastic system and to ordinate monks. The king, after consulting Thonmi Sambhota and other ministers sent an invitation to Śāntarakṣita to visit Tibet and establish Buddhist practices and monasteries.[1]

INTRODUCTION OF BUDDHISM

In the pages titled *Introduction of Buddhism in Tibet*, I have already described that the Śāntarakṣita's first attempt to introduce Buddhism in the land of the snow was a failure and after giving advice to the Tibetan king to invite Padmasambhava,[2] Śāntarakṣita was forced to return India. However, after the initial start up of Buddhism by Padmasambhava, Śāntarakṣita was invited again and this time he established the Samye monastery and remained Abbot of that monastery for whole thirteen years. He had done the work of assimilation of Bon practices with that of Buddhist practices and was endowed with different names by Tibetans, viz., *ācārya*, *bodhisattva*, and *mahāpaṇḍita*.[3] But lets have a look

1. Śāntarakṣita was the famous *ācārya* of that time. Due to non-Vedic tradition, his name may not be as famous as others but that time he was famous across Indian sub-continent (Jambūdvīpa).
2. In Tibetan he is called པདམ་འབྱུང་ནས། or པདམ་སམབྷ་བ། or གུ་རུ་རིན་པོ་ཆེ།
3. SCV, p. 323.

how Padmasambhava entered into Tibet for introducing Buddhism.

When Padmasambhava entered Tibet, the devil forces of Tibet welcomed him through the fire and snow streams. Getting unscathed, Padmasambhava successfully subdued the devil forces and their followers with the words that in Buddhism they will be given due share of their right from the people of Tibet. This was the first successful example of localization of Buddhism in Tibet. In addition, it was the stupendous assimilation of local faiths including Bon with the Buddhism to be adaptable in the distant region from the place of its origin.[4]

Padmasambhava

Padmasambhava, before leaving for Tibet, was the chief Abbot of the Oḍḍiyān monastery at Odantapurī. First of all, let us be clear that in the Mahāyāna Buddhism maintains that it is not only the Śākyamuni of the sixth century BC, i.e., the present *kalpa* who came to this world, attained Buddhahood (*nirvāṇa*=enlightenment) and passed away to the *mahāpari-nirvāṇa* stage, but the same school also says that in this world so many unaccountable individuals have attained *nirvāṇa* and *mahāparinirvāṇa* that their number can be compared with each sand particle laying in the bank of river Ganges. Yet, the number of predominantly recorded Buddha in the Mahāyāna texts is seven which in Tibetan is popularly known as སངས་རབ་བདུན or Sangye Rabdun or the Seven Buddhas. They are:

1. Vipāśu སངས་རྒྱས་རྣམ་པར་གཟིགས།
2. Śikhen སངས་རྒྱས་གཙུག་ཏོར་ཅན།
3. Viśvabhey སངས་རྒྱས་ཐམས་སྐྱོབས།
4. Krakuchanda སངས་རྒྱས་འཁོར་བ་གཟིགས།
5. Kanaka Muni སངས་རྒྱས་གསེར་ཐུབ།
6. Kaśyapa སངས་རྒྱས་འོད་སྲུངས།
7. Śākya Muni སངས་རྒྱས་ཤ་ཀྱ་ཐུབ་པ།

---

4. Bansal.

Hīnayāna primarily didn't accept the theory of countless Buddhas or *bodhisattva*, but after passage of time probably in later twentieth century accepted after some modification. Even till date the biggest assumption of Hīnayāna is that Gautama Buddha was a historic personality. On the other hand, the Mahāyāna continued to adopt the theory of countless Buddhas and *bodhisattva*s. It continued to follow its liberal theory and assimilation of the local believes that ultimately resulted in the complete localization of Buddhism in the area. The total outcome of this process brought the result that whichever country Buddhism entered; it changes its colour and appearances together with the rites and rituals; though the *Sūtra Piṭaka* and *Vinaya Piṭaka* continued being the source of authentication for any clarification. In my opinion, the theory of seven Buddhas was developed to establish that Buddhism is as old as the Vedic religion on Earth which at that time was considered the oldest and most authenticated one. So in every country the series of incarnation of Buddha occurred. This reached its extreme in Tibet where every important Lama is having his incarnation. In connection it is worth mentioning that Padmasambhava is known as the Buddha of Tantra. Mahāyāna tradition tells us that Lord Buddha himself couldn't teach Tantra because his body came out from mother womb. Since the Padmasambhava's body had come out from a Lotus, it was the purest one and hence authorized and capable to teach the Buddhist Tantra. It is so that Tantra is considered as the words of Buddha and is part of *Kanjur* in Tibetan Buddhism.

The Mahāyānist, particularly Nyingmapas believe that each of the seven Buddhas had made predictions during their lifetime that after their *mahāparinirvāṇa* there would appear in this world a super human being who, as a protector of Buddhism, would lead the sentient beings to the path of *nirvāṇa* as shown by the Buddha. It is further believed that the forecast of all these Buddha is embodied in one and the unique personality popularly known as the "Lord Padmasambhava" or "The Precious Guru" or "the lotus Born" came into this world.

Lord Padmasambhava has been appearing in this universe right from the time when the first Buddha came into being. In the present *kalpa* of Śākyamuni Buddha, it is firmly believed that the Buddha during his life time has predicted that twelve centuries after his *parinirvāṇa* there would appear a personality who would be much greater and mightier than the Buddha himself. Accordingly, in the seventh century AD there appeared in this world the "Lotus Born" who is the founder *guru* of Nyingma sect in Mahāyāna Buddhism.

Nyingma's Paths

The Nyingma Mahāyāna has two types of paths, Sūtra and Tantra. The great perfection (རྫོགས་ཆེན།) teaches both, but it itself is included within the Tāntric path. It contains the full meaning of all Sūtras and Tantras.

The thought of Buddha has three forms or in other words, Buddha has three bodies. They are: Truth Body (*dharmakāya*), Complete Enjoyment Body (*sambhogakāya*), and Emanation Body (*nirmāṇakāya*). The truth body is the body of emptiness that is beyond all elaborations of thought, the ultimate truth realised in full. The truth body, which is the nature of peace, has passed beyond all conceptions of object and subject; it is a state of having extinguished all celebrations of thought, and from its essence the body of complete enjoyment arises. The truth body is like a clear glass, and the light coming from it is the complete enjoyment body, a pure eternal manifestation in the form of highest truth. Emanations from the complete enjoyment body manifest in any form necessary to tame and help sentient beings. Each is an instance of an Emanation Body.

There are special female deities known as Mothers and Sky goers for whom this teaching is as precious as the essence of their own heart. To those who cherish it, it is known as the 'Heart Essence' (སྙིང་ཐིག།).

The preliminaries taught here are of two types: Common external and Special internal preparations. Both are prerequisite practices for final teaching in accordance with the doctrine of the great perfection or Dzog Chen (*atiyoga*).

There are two types of realisation in Nyingma tradition, visionary and cognitive, and within the visionary, there are many different types. However, the important among others are the visions of appearance, emptiness and bliss. Just as there are objects that appear to our eye consciousness, in the same way there are many objects which appear to our mental consciousness. These are visions of appearance. The factors or objects appearing to a consciousness without an inherently existent subject and object being posited, are the vision of emptiness. When the vision of emptiness — "the absence of the signs of subject and object" — is seen, bliss is generated within the person and this is the vision of bliss.

Transmission of Teachings

In Nyingma, there are three transmissions: Transmission through the Conqueror's thought, through the symbols of knowledge-bearers, and through ears. The transmission through the conqueror's thought passes directly from the complete enjoyment body, the pure eternal manifestation of the truth, to the trainee. This is the case of mental transmission where one being transmits his thoughts to another directly without words and symbols. The complete enjoy-ment body, which in this case is Sāmantabhadra, transfers whatever he knows directly to the minds of his disciples. Disciples who appear directly to a Buddha can receive such instruction or teachings.

The second transmission is through the symbols of knowledge bearers. When thought cannot be directly transmitted, it is necessary to depend on symbols. For example, at a crossroad there are signs indicating directions; through seeing them you know where to go. There are no words involved; you understand them through certain arrangements of colours and shapes. Vajradhara himself transmitted understanding to his disciples by using signs and symbols. He originated his transmission, and five different types of beings — gods, dragons, demons, Lichhavis and Yakṣas — passed on the transmission after receiving it from him. Knowledge-bearers, those who have assimilated the knowledge of suchness in their minds, transmit through this tradition. Knowledge of suchness, the immutable nature of all objects is the mean to escape from the cyclic existence; without this knowledge, one is trapped.

For those who cannot understand the teaching transmitted through signs and symbols there is transmission through ears. Here the teacher's thought is expressed in words which enter the ear. How is the teaching done? One way is through empowering blessings, another through hearing scriptures and a third method is through initiation. Depending on this type of transmission, one engages in practice and actualization of truth.

According to Nyingma tradition, there are nine vehicles. A vehicle is a system of practice by which one progresses to a higher state. The nine vehicles are arranged into three groups consisting of three sub-groups each. The three external ones leading away from the source of cyclic existence are those meant for Hearers, Solitary Realisers and Bodhisattvas (श्रावकयान, प्रत्येकबुद्धयान और बोधिसत्वयान). The three inner ones involving all types of asceticism are the three lower Tantras; Action performance and Yoga (*kriyā, caryā,* and *yoga*).[5] The three secret vehicles serving as methods of empowerment are *mahāyoga, anuyoga* and *atiyoga*. Patrul Rinpochey pays homage to Jig-Me-Ling-Pa who illuminated *atiyoga,* the highest of all systems of practice for developing the mind. It is also made famous by another name Dzog Chen practices.

Buddha's teaching is of two types, verbal and realized. The former consists of words detailing excellent qualities of mind and practices for attaining them. The latter are

5. Wayman.

realizations attained through following the verbal teaching just as it is. Therefore, the actual teaching of Buddha is identified by these two, whereas books and common teachers whom we can meet are just conventional instructors.

Nyingma Concept of Bodhisattva

A *bodhisattva* resolves: I take upon myself the burden of all suffering, I am resolved to do so, and I will endure it. I do not turn to run away, do not tremble, am not terrified or afraid and do not turn back or despond.

And why? At all costs, I must bear the burden of all beings, in that I do not follow my own inclinations. I have made the vow to save all beings. All beings I must set free. The whole world of living beings must I rescue. From the terror of birth, of old age, of sickness, of death and rebirth, of all kinds of moral offence, of all state of woe, of the whole cycle of birth and death, of the jungle of false views, of the loss of wholesome *dharma*s, of the concomitants of ignorance, from all these terrors, I must rescue all beings. I walk so that the kingdom of unsurpassed cognition is built up for all beings. My endeavours do not merely aim at my own deliverance. For with the help of the boat of the thought of all-knowledge, I must rescue all these beings from the stream of *saṁsāra*, which is so difficult to cross, I must pull them back from the great precipice, I must free them from all calamities. I must ferry them across the stream of *saṁsāra*. I myself must grapple with the whole mass of suffering of all beings. To the limit of my endurance, I will experience in all the states of woe, found in any world system and in all the abodes of suffering. In addition, I must not cheat all beings out of my store of merit. I am resolved to abide in each single state of woe for numberless aeons; and so I will help all beings to freedom, in all the states of woe that may be found in any world system whatsoever.

And why? Because it is surely better that I alone should be in pain than that all these beings should fall into the states of wretchedness. There I must give myself a way as a pawn through which the whole world is redeemed from the terrors of the hells, of animal birth, of the world of Yama, and with this my own body I must experience, for the sake of all beings, the whole mass of all painful feelings. And on behalf of all beings I give surety for all beings, and in doing so I speak truthfully, am trustworthy, and do not go back on my word. I must not abandon all beings.

And why? There has arisen in me the will to win all knowledge, with all beings for its object, that is to say, for the purpose of settings free the entire world of beings. And I have not set out for the supreme enlightenment from a desire for delights, not because I hope to experience the delights of the five sense-qualities, or because I wish to indulge in the pleasures of the senses. Moreover, I do not pursue the course of a *bodhisattva* in order to achieve the array of delights that can be found in the various worlds of sense-desire.

And why? Truly, no delights are all these delights of the world. All this indulging in the pleasures of the senses belongs to the sphere of Māra (Satan of Buddhism).

Doctrine of Nirvāṇa

The Nyingma School teaches that neither spirit nor substance nor law (*karma*), in organised life is self-created (*svabhāvasiddha*). These are in mutual relation, and therefore exist only in virtue of such relationship; but by synthesizing them we came to the concept of *śūnyatā*, the absolute unchangeable being which is also found in other religious order by the different name, viz., Ākāśa, God, etc. The Buddha Vajrasattva in the Mahāyāna school is an approach to typify the Absolute, the self-created called *svabhāvasiddha*. In the Tāntric Buddhism of Tibet "Yab dang Yum" the patriarch, with his wife and child, typifies the Trinity, the Logos or the word as known to us or manifested to humanity as God the Father; God the Mother, and God the son. Metaphysically there are spirits, substances and divine law of *karma*; none of these and neither organized life is self-created, or *svabhāvasiddha*. In the plane of manifestation there is neither permanence nor reality — it is not the plane of "enduring substance." Let us analyse any object of scene, as a house. What is the house? Take all its parts: door, roof, etc., the house is none of them, nor it is the sum total of them. Nor it is other than them. It only exists in relation of the parts and in name: therefore it is not *svabhāvasiddha*, or self-created. This is the core doctrine of Buddhism: The doctrine of *pratītyasamutpāda* or the theory of dependent origination (རྟེན་ཆེན་འབྲེལ་འབྱུང་།), in other words made existent through relation and evolution. Consistently with this doctrine, Buddhists do not believe in the existence of a creator. Therefore, there cannot be a creation. According to them, the world has existed from the infinite time (eternity), the living beings in it also exist from the time infinite, and so spirit and substances are co-eternal. The indivisible spirit (*ātmā*), like absolute matter or atom, cannot cease to exist. Their quantity cannot be diminished or increased. Of this world not one real particle or atom (as distinguished from phenomenon matter) can be lost. Therefore, there is no such word as annihilation in the Buddhist terminology. In my opinion, this theory of Buddhism in closely related to the theory of conservation of energy in Physics that is a proven fact in natural sciences. Hence, to say that Buddhism is the most logical religion in the world and scientific in approach will not be an exaggeration. One can think well that the Buddhist masters taught and practised the theory of conservation of energy in the sixth century BC!

An animate being, called *sattva* (organized life) is a compound in which spirit and substance arte combined, being intimately connected together by a force called in Sanskrit *karma* (ལས། in Tibetan). It is possible for the spirit to become apparently separate from substance, or at the time of each dissolution of the body called "Death." After each such separation, the force of *karma* attracts the spirit that remains inherent in it, to a fresh organized existence, be it that of a god, demon, ghost, or hell-being in which existence is corporeal though in some cases, the body may be fine and in other gross.

Now, this force of *karma* is of a mixed character. It is qualified by the moral actions of the animate being, i.e., by the action of the animate being in the relation to the other animate beings. If the moral act is selfish, i.e., if it is drawn towards its own self or self-interest, called *svārtha* (བདག་འཛིན།) or ego, which leads to sin it will get a firm hold of the self so as to enchain it to matter. On the other hand, if the *karma* is unselfish or drawn towards the interest of others, i.e., to *parārtha*, or Altruism, which leads to virtue, then it will gradually loose its hold on the self. The *karma* that leads to sin is like water coloured with a dark tincture; the *karma* that leads to virtue from the absence of sin is like pure water, colourless.

The *ātmā* or spirit then moves towards the state of *mukti* (ཐར་པ།), or liberation from the phenomenal matter, i.e., the state of sin. The *karma* that enchains the self of spirit to the body is called sin, and sin leads to utter darkness called *avidyā* (རྨོངས་པ). The *karma* that gives it freedom (*mukti*) is called virtue. It takes the spirit to *bodhi* or enlightenment. When the spirit is free from sin and fully in virtue, it is called Sāmantabhadra (in Nyingma tradition), the All-good-God (ཀུན་ཏུ་བཟང་པོ།) or the Buddha (སངས་རྒྱས། in Tibetan), the perfectly purified one. So a Buddha is evolved, set free from worldliness and organized existence, gross or fine. Buddha is purely spiritual entity, enlightened or sublimed by virtue or good *karma*.

During the reign of King Khri Srong Dehu Tsan (around AD 730) the Chinese way to practice Buddhism was intro-duced by Hashang. The doctrine was the path of sudden enlightenment. Nevertheless, it contained the doctrine of absolute inactivity, or what is vulgarly called, "so Nothing." He taught that to obtain the state of perfect emancipation from transmigratory existence, the spirit should be free from the any type of *karma* or action. Hashang further argued that as long as there is any *karma*, be it virtuous or sinful the spirit

(གང་ཟག) would remain in bondage to transmigatory existence. Therefore, to get out of it one should neither commit sin nor practice virtue, as both of these would equally entangle one to worldliness and matter. The best course, therefore, for attending *nirvāṇa* according to Hashang was to do nothing. This Buddhist teacher was expelled from Tibet after his defeat in a debate with the Indian philosopher Kamalaśīla, who happened to be in Tibet at that time.

During countless ages of the world, countless Buddhas have thus, gone to the state of perfectly purity — not one Buddha only, as is generally believed. The Buddha are therefore called *tathāgatas*, meaning Thus gone, or Thus came (तथा+गत and तथ+आगत), i.e., *viśuddhi* (absolute purity). *Viśuddhi* is synonym to *nirvāṇa*, and *viśuddhimārga* means the way to *nirvāṇa*. In the present *kalpa* (Age), [which on account of the supposed appearance of the seven Buddhas], is called the Glorious Age, there will appear, according to Do-Kal-Sang (མདོ་སྐལ་བཟང་།) a thousand more Buddhas; owing to this auspicious circumstances this great period of time is called *bhadra kalpa*, i.e., the glorious Age.

It is said that the when animate beings of the world will begin to move towards sin, by aiming at material prosperity and sensual happiness, then no Buddha will appear, it will take them long time to attain the state of celestial beings such as Indra, Brahmā and other Gods, and as they should do to further purification and enlightenment. In consequence of the downward tendencies of all human beings, that time is called "Dark Period." The position of gods and duration of the periods of their bliss, are collapsed, as in the case of human beings, but not the extent of their moral merits, that is to say, the merits they showed when they lived as men on earth, or in some sphere, not heaven. Thus the wheel of life turns — Indra, Brahmā and others who were once gods in heaven may today be ordinary mortal men in exalted or in lowly sphere of life; and vice versa. The turn of the great wheel which one day exalts men to gods in heaven and another day brings down gods to be men on earth explains two great truths, on of which is frequently lost sight of. We believe in general, what all scriptures teach essentially, the divinity of man or, the "god" upon earth; but we do not so generally believe in the often equally necessary truth, viz., the humanity of god. After exhaustion of the merits with which terminates his celestial bliss, he has to revert to his former position, or to a worse state in this world. Therefore, it is foolish on the part of man to lay out so much of his merits in the wrong direction instead of utilizing the same to the right end: ensuring his attaiment of the state of Bodhi, of enlightenment.

Lamaism

The Lord Padmasambhava usually called Padmajungne or Guru Rinpoche by the Tibetans founded Lamaism. Lamaism arose in the time of Khri Song Dehu Tsan whose rule was from AD 740 to 786. The son of a Chinese princess, he inherited from his mother a strong prejudice in favour of Buddhism. He was sent to India for books and teachers. In addition, commenced a systematic translation from the Sanskrit and Chinese scriptures; and he built the first Buddhist Monastery in Tibet which is known as Samye.

It was in connection with the construction of this monastery the Padmasambhava came to Tibet, with an invitation of the Tibetan king Khri Song Dehu Tsan. All the king's endeavours to build the monastery were confronted by the Earthquakes that were attributed to demons. On the advice of the Indian Buddhist monk Śāntarakṣita, a letter was sent to the great Indian monastery of Nālandā for the wizard-priest Padmasambhava of the Yogācāra School, who was a famous sorcerer. Padmasambhava, who was a native of Uḍḍyāna, or Ghazani, a region famous for sorcery, promptly responded to the Tibetan king's request and arrived at Samye, by the way of Kāṭhmāṇḍu and Kyirong in Nepal. It was the year AD 747 and Padmasambhava reached with Dorje or thunderbolt and magic spells from Mahāyāna school of Nālandā. He vanquished and converted the devils, built the monastery in AD 749 and established the first community of Lamaism.

Lamaism may be defined as a mixture of Buddhism with a preponderating amount of mythology, mysticism and magic. The doctrine of incarnate Lamas and the worship of canalized saints now is one of the most prominent features of Lamaism in Tibet and the Tibetan are famous worldwide by this practice. It was readily accepted as it protected the people from devils.

Importance of Faith in Nyingma Sect (དད་པ།)

Taking refuge in triple jewels — Buddha, Dharma and Saṅgha, is the foundation of all Buddhist paths and in another way the answer for the question; to whom we may call a Buddhist. Naturally, one who took refuge in three jewels (or triple gems, as some name them) is a Buddhist.

Faith is of three types: Clarity, Desire to attain and knowledgeable conviction. When we see an image or meet a teacher, we are overwhelmed with as feeling of *āhā*, "how nice this is," "how wonderful," etc. This is the faith of clarity; the mind is clear and receptive.

The desire to attain means seeking something special; qualities that we have heard about, such as the compassion, love and wisdom of *bodhisattva*s, etc. It can also signify a wish to be free from the sufferings of cyclic existence, or to engage in virtues and relinquish non-virtues. Through learning about the qualities of Buddha, his Dharma and the Saṅgha we can come to generate a desire to attain them.

The faith of conviction is, for instance, the knowledge that the three jewels are a suitable sources of refuge. It is a seed generating these excellent qualities. If we are bothered by doubt, it is like having a seed that has been burned; it can still sprout, but it cannot grow properly and its seed will be black like smoke. It is said that without faith of conviction it is very difficult to generate any auspicious qualities.

Faith is like a wheel, always ready to roll along the road. If we have it, we can make internal progress at any time. Faith is an inexhaustible treasure of good qualities. It is a vehicle carrying us along the path to omniscience, an outstretched hand drawing us to all good qualities.

The extent to which spiritual qualities can be internalized depends on faith. If it is floundering, so are the qualities developed; if immeasurable, so too will be the attainments.

Buddha's personal attendant Ānanda, who remained with him for many years (about 25 years continuously), was not able to generate any of the master's qualities because he lacked faith. When we have great faith, its benefit remains no matter how far away we may be from Buddha or our lama (*guru*).

It is said that if we have faith, Padmasambhava will sit by our door while we are asleep. The tutor of the Fifth Dalai Lama once entered his pupil's room through the window.

"Why have you come in through the window?" Dalai Lama asked.

"There was no other way since one Nyingmapa lama is sleeping at your door." The tutor replied. He was referring to the Dalai Lama's strong faith in the Nyingma trans-mission.

For one who has faith, even the tooth of a dog can bring blessings. If someone cherishes it as the tooth of Buddha — whether, he has been deceived or simply mistaken — he will receive as much benefit as the actual Buddha's tooth bestows.

A simple fellow with great faith visited Lhasa in order to see the image of Jo-Bo Rinpoche in the main temple. He saw the food offering made by others and thought that they were meant to be eaten by the image — which he took to be an actual person — and him. He helped himself to a small portion and mixed it with the butter from one of the lamps lighted there in the temple. A group of dogs then ran through the temple and made off with Jo-Bo Rinpoche's food. That person was filled with admiration at the way the marvellous lama (the statue) smiled calmly at it all through. The wind began blowing through the doors and nearly snuffed out the butter lamps, and again the fellow marvelled at how the Lama could simply sit and smile at it all. He wanted to perform the circumambulation of the temple of this wonderful Lama, but first he put off his shoes and respectfully placed them in the begging bowl on the Lama's lap.

While he was performing the circumambulation outside, the keeper of the temple passed by the altar and saw the shoes in the image's begging bowl.

"Ah, these dirty shoes" he exclaimed and tried to throw them away, but he was suddenly stopped by a command from the image.

"Leave them here." When that simple fellow returned and saw his shoes safe in the begging bowl, he praised Jo-Bo-Rinpoche,

"Oh, you are such a fine lama; you have kept my shoes for me. Please come and visit me," he said to the image, "I will kill a pig for you and heat up some beer; we will have a fine feast."

Due to his good thought, the image answered,

"Yes, I will surely come."

The fellow returned home and told his family that he had met a very great lama who had accepted an invitation to visit him. He ordered his family.

"I do not know when he will come, so please look out for him." One day his wife went to fetch water from a nearby spring and in it saw a reflection of the lama. She ran home and called her husband.

"Your visitor has come, but he has fallen into the water. Please go out and help him."

The man rushed out to the spring and saw Jo-Bo-Rinpoche.

"Oh, the great lama has fallen into the water," he cried and jumped in without hesitation. He helped the Lama out and exclaimed, "you have had so much difficulty getting here. Please come with me and I will offer you meat and beer."

On the way to his home the Lama stopped and said, "I cannot enter a lay person's home, I must return to my temple," and disappeared into a nearby rock. The fellow then set the meat and beer out before the rock, which displayed an image of Jo-Bo-Rinpoche.

The Tibetans still make offerings at the spring, now called Jo-Bo spring, and the rock where these events took place. Even though a statue is itself incapable of appearing as a living being, it did so because of the great faith of this simple man. Faith can force the Buddha to appear in person before the devotee. It is said that if you have faith in Buddha, Dharma and Saṅgha, the door to refuge will open and you will be able to enter all the numerous paths that the dharma contains.

The Daily Routine of a Lama of Nyingma Sect

The Nyingma monk has to perform according to the tradition of Nyingma sect. The monk immediately on waking must arise from his bed even though it is midnight and commence to chant མི་རྟག་སྒོམ་འཛུགས། taking care to pronounce all the words fully and distinctly. This contains the instruction of his especial Lama preceptor of root Lama རྩ་བའི་བླ་མ། and in the recital; the monk must call vividly to mind his spiritual guide. This is followed by a prayer for a number of requests by the monk himself. Then he assumes the meditative posture of the seven "attitudes," in order to subjugate the five senses. These attitudes are:

1. Sitting with the leg flexed in the well-known attitude of Buddha.
2. The one hand rested above the other in the lap.
3. Head slightly bent forwards.
4. Eyes fixed on the tip of the nose.

5. Shoulder "flouting like wing of a vulture."
6. Spine erected straight like an arrow.
7. Tongue arched towards the palate like the carving petals of the eight-levelled-lotus.

While in this posture he must think that he is along in a wilderness.

The three original sins of the body, i.e., lust, anger and slothfulness are then got rid of the humeral pathology of the ancient in the three series of Buma, Roma and Kyangma (འབུ་མ།རོ་མ།དང་རྐྱང་མ།). This will be done after taking a deep inspiration, the air of the Roma veins is expelled three times, and this "the white winds" is laid out from the right nostril three times in short and forcible expiratory guest. This expels all anger. Then from the left nostril is thrice expelled in a smaller way "The Red air," which rids lust. The colourless central air is thrice expelled which frees from ignorance. On concluding this process, the monk must mentally realise of all that ignorance, lust and anger — the three original sins have disappeared like frost before a scorching sun. Thereafter they say "Al-alia-li" keeping the tongue curved like a lotus petal. This is followed by his chanting the "Yoga of the Lama" (བླ་མའི་རྣལ་འབྱོར།), during which he must mentally conceive his Lama — Guide as seating overhead upon lotus flower. Then assuring the spiritual guise of his Yidam of tutelary deity (ཡི་དམ), he chants the four-preliminary-services — the སྔོན་འགྲོ་བཞི་འབྱོར།. These are the refuge formed or སྐྱབས་འགྲོ, which cleanses the darkness of the body, the hindered letters of ཡིག་བརྒྱ, which cleanses all obscurity in speech; and the magic circle of the rice — the *maṇḍala* which cleanses the mind; and the prayer གསོལ་འདེབས། clarifying lamas up to the most perfect one, conjures perfection on the monk himself. This is followed by the chanting of the བླ་སྒྲུབ། or "the obtaining of the Lamas," and the "the obtaining of the ornaments Sang Dup."

The deity in this worship is called "The agreeable One" (ཞི་བ།) and the demon དྲག་པོ། is called "The Repulsive."

The demonical form must recited the full number of lines which the Lamas bound him to do by vow before his spiritual tutor, viz., 100, 1000 or 10,000 times daily. Those not bound in this way by vows repeat the charm as many times as they conveniently can.

Having done this, he may retire again to sleep, if the night be not very far advanced. Nevertheless, if the dawn is near, he must not go to sleep, but employ the interval in several sorts of prayer called སྨོན་ལམ།. As soon as day dawns, he must wash his face and rinse his mouth and do the worship above noted, should he not have already done so.

Then he takes his breakfast and meals. If there be any *stūpa* (ཆོས་རྟེན) or monastery near at hand, then he will go there with prayer wheel at his hand. In the evening, he will repeat some མཐུན= circumbulance (प्रदक्षिणा) and at 9.00 or 10.00 p.m., he sleeps.

A devotee of Nyingma Lama follows this practice religiously unto his death.

Accumulation of Virtue

(༄༅།།བསོད་ནམས་ཀྱི་ཚོགས།།)

A *bodhisattva*, great compassionate being, considers the world with its ten directions, in every direction, extending everywhere. He considers the world systems, quite calm and immeasurable, quite beyond reckoning, quite measureless, quite inconceivable, and infinite and boundless.

He considers in the past period, in each single direction, in each single world system, the *tathāgatas*, quite immeasurable, quite beyond reckoning, quite measureless, quite inconceivable, infinite and boundless, who have one final *nirvāṇa* in the realm of *nirvāṇa* that leaves nothing behind, their tracks cut-off, their courses cut-off, they obstacles annulled, guides through (the world of) becoming, their tears dried up, with all their impediments crashed, their own burdens laid down, with their own weal reached, in whom the fetters of becoming are extinguished, whose thoughts are well freed by right understanding, and who have attained the highest perfection in the control of their hearts.

He considers them, from where they began with the production of the thought of enlightenment, proceeding to the time when they won full enlightenment, until they finally entered *nirvāṇa* in the realm of *nirvāṇa* that leaves nothing behind and the whole span of the time up to the vanishing of the good *dharma* (as preached by one of these *tathāgata*s).

He considers the mass of morality, the mass of concentration, the mass of wisdom, the mass of emancipation, the mass of the vision and of cognition of emancipation of these Buddhas and Lords.

In addition he considers the store of merit associated with the six perfections, with the achievement of the qualities of a Buddha, and with the perfection of self-confidence and of the powers; and also those associated with the perfection of the super knowledge, of comprehension of the vows; and the store of the merit associated with the accomplishment of the cognition of the all knowing, with the solicitude of beings the great friendliness, great compassion and the immeasurable and incalculable Buddha-qualities.

Also the full enlightenment and its happiness, the perfection of the sovereignty over all *dharma*s, the accomplishment of the measurable unconquered, supreme wonder working power which has conquered all, and the power of the *tathāgata*'s cognition of what is truly real, which is equal to the unequalled, incomparable, without measure, the power of the Buddha-cognition pre-eminent among the powers, the vision and cognition of a Buddha, the obtainment of that supreme ease which results from the four grounds of self-confidence and the obtainment of *dharma* through the realization of the ultimate reality of all *dharma*s.

He also considers the turning of the wheel of *dharma*, the carrying of its torch, beating of its drum, filling-up and sounding of its conch-shell, wielding of its sword, the pouring down of the rain of *dharma*, the offering of the sacrifice of *dharma*, the refreshment of all beings through the gift of *dharma* through its presentation to them. He further considers the store of merit of all those who are educated and trained by those demonstrations of *dharma*, whether they concern the *dharma*s of Buddhas, or those of *pratyekabuddha*s, or of disciples, who believe in them, who are fixed on them or who are bound to end up in full enlightenment.

He also considers the store of merit, associated with the six perfections, of all those *bodhisattva*s who belong to the *pratyekabuddha*-vehicle, and of whom the enlightenment of a *pratyekabuddha* has been predicted. He considers the meritorious work deciphered on giving, morality and meditative development of those who belong to the disciple-vehicle, and the roots of good with blemish, for those who are still in training as well as the unblemished roots of good of the adepts.

He considers the roots of good, which the common people have planted as a result of the teaching of those *tathāgata*s. He considers the meritorious work, underlying morality and meditative development, of the four assemblies of Buddhas and Lords, i.e., of the monks, and nuns, the laymen and laywomen. He considers the roots of good planted during all that time by gods, *nāgas*, *yakṣas*, *gandharvas*, *asuras*, *garuḍas*, *kinnaras* and *mahoragas*, by men and ghosts, and also by animals. At the time when those Buddhas and lords demonstrated the *dharma*s, and when they entered *parinirvāṇa* — thanks to the Buddhas, the Lord, thanks to the *dharma*, and thanks to the *saṅgha*, and thanks to persons of right mind-cultures (in this meditation the *bodhisattva*). The *bodhisattva* piles up the roots of goods of all those, all those qualities of merit without exception or remainder, rolls it into one lamp, lights it, and rejoices over it with the most excellent and sublime jubilation, the highest and utmost jubilation, with none above it, unequalled equalling the unequalled. Having thus rejoiced, he would utter the remark,

"I turn over into full enlightenment the meritorious work founded on jubilation. May it feed the full enlightenment (of me and of all beings)."

Bhāvacakra: Its Significance

BHĀVACAKRA OR "THE CYCLIC EXISTENCE"

(སྲིད་པའི་འཁོར་ལོ།)

In *bhāvacakra* chart, we can all the time see a monster holding the "Wheel of Existence." The monster in whose grip the whole universe is, typifies Egoism or selfishness called བདག་འཛིན།. According to the Mahāyāna school of Buddhism, freedom from the grasp of this monster is freedom from the suffering of all minds and attaining of *nirvāṇa*, in other word salvation of altruism. If we look at the picture of *bhāvacakra*, there human birth being considered as the best and happiest state of existence, is placed at the top of the six states.

The existence, i.e., the state of the moral Gods such as Indra, Brahmā, etc., being considered inferior to that of humanity; placed on its right and immediately below the human birth. The unhappy state of the *asura*s of demi-gods is placed to the left of the humanity. The *nāga*s or serpent demi-gods, are included in the fourth state, i.e., that of the *tiryak* including beasts, birds, reptiles, insects, worms and, etc., in the section *preta*s or ghosts, i.e., the names of the dead, are put in the face state called the state of unhappy.

The last and lowest state is that of the hell beings. All the six states are evolved out of humanity (as represented in the outer circle) by the force called *karma* (i.e., good or bad actions) which is continually at work keeping them in motion. This force cannot be annihilated by any power but may be regulated to better purpose.

The outer ring of the plate contains a circular road one half of which is white and the other half black. The white portion marked is the path of Deity (*sagati*); the black part is the way to sin (*dugati*). At the lowest end of the white road stands a man of the world carrying on his back a load of sacred volumes. By merit of carrying the volumes he moves one step forward in piety and learns the mystic syllabus, *oṁ-maṇi-padme-huṁ* and turns the prayer wheel containing numberless inscriptions of (*oṁ-maṇi-padme-huṁ*). He then becomes a monk shaving his head and gives up the worldly life to enter into a religious life, i.e., that of Lama. Being admitted as a novice priest, he carries on horse back a *caitya* or some sacred volumes. In the meantime, he becomes tired of a religious life and wishes to become a high government official. He is presently appointed as the Minister of State of the Grand Lama, or Flag bearer or the carrier of his incense pot, but at last finding out his mistake, he reverts to his former position in the monastery. Taking the image of the Buddha in the right-hand and a lamp in his left hand, he performs religious services. In old age, he becomes a hermit. While verging on death he is permitted to truth either the way to *nirvāṇa* by drinking nectar from the Tshei Bumpa (ཚེའི་བུམ་པ།) or the pot of life offered to him by *bodhisattva* (བྱང་ཆུབ་སེམས་པ), or to enter worldly life of humanity of the gods or demigods by eating the fruit held to him by the incarnate saint who stands at the top of the white path. As soon as he tastes of the *phalam*, i.e., the forbidden fruit, he falls headlong on the black path of sin where adversity in her various forms of demons, drags him mercilessly up and down. The pious man, who has chosen a religious life by drinking from the pot of life, takes the vows of *bodhisattva* and gains higher spiritual status. Though still in the world he ceases to be a man of the world, he does well to all living beings, unselfishly and gradually conquering the three enemies, unselfishly *kāma* (འདོད་ཆགས།), *krodha* (ཞྭག་སྡོག།) and *moha* (གཏི་མུག།) (typified cock, snake and pig in the picture in the centre) completely, he becomes an immortal God of Jina or Victorious. He then becomes perfectly free from the grasp of selfishness (ང་རྒྱལ།). The monster symbolizes moral death.

The erring man choosing to enjoy the *phalam* (fruit) of his merits returns as a king, minister, merchant or householder to the world. It is he who likes it, then according to his liking, takes birth in celestial region to become a mortal god like Brahmā or Indra. At the expiration of his merits or concurrently while enjoying the fruit of his merit, on account of his sins he is born as a demon, beast, *nāga,* insect or hell-worm or a *preta.* All these states of existence are in his lot which he travels in the round path of piety and sin. There still he has opportunity of choosing to go to the peaceful state of immortality, i.e., *nirvāṇa,* or to the states of sufferings and sorrow in (*kāma loka*), the world of desire.

The process of recurring existence of sorrow and pain are explained by 12 *nidāna*s as:

1. *Avidyā* — Ignorance typified by a blind man.
2. *Saṁskāra* — Typified by a potter and pots (creation).
3. *Vijñāna* — Consciousness (restless soul) typified by the monkey.
4. *Nāma-Rūpa* — Typified by the Noah's ark containing a man + woman + animal.
5. *Ṣaḍāyatana* — Typified by the empty house containing doors, windows, etc., symbolical of the sense-organs.
6. *Sparśa* (Contact) — Typified by the husband and wife embracing each other.
7. *Vedanā* (Sensation) — of delusive pleasure and pain typified by an arrow entering a man's eye.
8. *Tṛṣṇā* — Strong Desire for the worldly enjoyments is represented by a man drinking wine and a woman holding the wine-jug to replenish his cup.
9. *Upādāna* — Indulgence of desire typified by a man collecting fruits and storing them in a basket.
10. *Bhāva* — Conception of human birth typified by man and woman in the state of copulation.
11. *Jāti* — Birth from the womb typified by the very birth of a child from the womb.

12. *Maraṇa* — Death typified by the last journey of a corpse carried on the back of a coolie to the cemetery.

Buddha, out of his compassion for all living beings of this world manifests himself as a teacher in each of the six states of existence. The immortal God Lokeśvara called Mahākāruṇika interprets the *dharma* (law) by sending emanation of his spirit to all the six states.

Looking at the circle we find twelve pictures. The cause of re-birth — the *nidānas* — are categorically given as twelve in the form of a linked chain, the result of the first cause being the cause of the second and so on; the ultimate result being suffering.

These illustrations with their lamaic paraphrases are:

I. A blind old woman groping her way is མ་རིག་པ། or "Want of knowledge," which is the cardinal cause of existence, leading people to mistake for happiness the miseries of existence.

II. A potter with his wheel making pots *saṁskāra* (འདུ་བྱེད།) or "impressing"— literally "preparation or fashioning + action", showing the fruits of worldly labour are perishable objects — action being misdirected as a result of ignorance.

III. A monkey is eating fruit; *vijñāna* (རྣམ་པར་ཤེས་པ) or "entire knowledge" of good and evil fruits — tasting every fruit in the sense of a roving libertine without system; thus engendering consciousness.

IV. A dying man with a physician feeling pulse (in some other illustration there will be boat with passengers being ferried across the water; ocean of existence), is *nāma-rūpa*, name and form (མིང་དང་གཟུགས།) is human being. Its fleeting character is shown by the man being about to lose his individuality and name in death.

V. An empty house is *ṣaḍāyatana* (སྐྱེ་ས་མཆེད་དྲུག།) or "The five mortal senses organs and mind", illustrated the organs and the will which are the result of individual being — the hollowness of these is typified.

VI. A pair of lovers kissing — *sparśa* (རེག་པ།) or contact which results from the exercise of the sense-organs and will.

VII. An arrow entering a man's eye is *vedanā* (ཚོར་བ།) or perception, the result of a contact. It includes joy and sorrow as well as pain.

VIII. A man drinking wine *tṛṣhṇā* (སྲེད་པ།) or desire for more, including thirst and affection, which result from the exercise of perceptive faculty.

IX. A man gathering a large basket full of flowers. *Upādāna* (ལེན་པ།) or taking; grasping indulgence in worldly matters — the result is desire.

X. A pregnant woman — *bhāva* (སྲིད་པ།) or continuity of existence, a desire for inheritance — the result of clinging to worldly life and wealth.

XI. A mother in childbirth — *jāti* (སྐྱེ་བ།) or birth as a result of *bhāva*.

XII. A human corpse being carried off is *jarā maraṇa* (.རྒ་བ་དང་ཤི་བ།) or decay and death with all their sufferings, which are the result of birth.

4

The Tertons
A Unique Tradition in NyingMa[1]

People, who have well-being of mind, even if the Buddha is not present, will receive dharma from the midst of the sky, walls and trees. For that bodhisattva whose minds are pure, teachings and instructions will appear just by the wishes in their minds. — Buddha[2]

Meaning of gTer

In a great number of spiritual traditions of the world, there are many instances of the discovery of teachings and objects by mystical power. Similarly, in various traditions and lineages of Buddhism, in India as well as Tibet, numerous discoveries of teachings and objects have taken place.

In the Nyingma school of Tibetan Buddhism the tradition of concealment and revelations of teachings and materials of religious value through the mystical power of enlightened beings is most prevalent. This tradition of mystical discovery is known in Tibet as གཏེར (treasures), གཏེར་མ (treasured ones), or གཏེར་ཆོས, *dharma* treasures of Treasured teachings.

Ter does not belong to the category of revelations through psychic power (ཏྲ་ཁམས) or through the beings of the spirit world (མི་མ་ཡིན). Psychic discoveries take place through the power of

---

1. ལས་འཕྲོ་གཏེར་བརྒྱུད་ཀྱི་རྣམ་བཤད་ངོ་མཚར་རྒྱ་མཚོ་ by the third Dodrupchen Jigmed Ten poi Nyingma (1865-1926).

2. ADS, p. 84b.

mind, which is a gifted but conceptual cognition. Further, most spirits have more physical power and knowledge than ordinary human beings, but their spiritual wisdom and true virtues are limited. The discoveries of Terma take place from the omnipresent enlightened nature of mind through the spontaneously arisen wisdom power of the enlightened nature itself whereas other discoveries are through dualistic concepts and supernatural deeds.

In Mahāyāna Buddhism in general and especially in Tantra the true nature of the universe is viewed as the ultimate peace, emptiness, openness, the enlightened, awakened state, bliss, oneness, freedom from dualistic concepts and the wisdom of knowing all simultaneously, and that is known as the state fully enlightened nature of Buddha. Mahāyānists including *tāntric*s believe that the true nature of the mind of beings is pure as Buddha but that has been obscured by wrong views, emotions and habits. We are distracted into dualistic phenomena and thus are trapped in the unending turmoil of the mundane world.

Hevajra Tantra (KYe'i-RDo-RJe-RGYud) says:

> Beings are Buddha in their nature,
> But their nature is obscured by adventitious defilements.
> When the defilements are cleansed they themselves
> Are the very Buddha

If you attain freedom from the mind of grasping at the selfless phenomena as "self" and transcend dualistic perception through spiritual trainings, then the whole universe before you merges into the oneness of great peace. That is the attainment of Buddhahood, the absolute nature. If you attain Buddhahood, then every activity becomes the spontaneously arisen Buddha-action. All phenomenons appear and are seen through the omniscient Buddha wisdom, as they are: simultaneous and without discriminations, limitations and dualities. You (We usually) see all through the all-knowing wisdom of neither Buddha nature, nor through the dualistic conceptual mind.

According to Buddhist Tantras, in order to bring an ordinary person to the realization of the enlightened nature, it is very important for the person to receive the transmission of the power of blessings of the realization (རྟོགས་པའི་བྱིན་རླབས) from a realized master. Then such a lineage of transmission moves through stages and times as the link to the realization, the true awakened nature, and as the means of communication of the teachings.

The main tradition of Terma tradition of the Nyingma School is Guru Padmasambhava. He was one of the greatest *tāntric* masters and saints of Buddhist history. In the ninth century AD, at the invitation of Tibetan King, he came to Tibet from India and fulfilled three major missions. First, through the display of spiritual power, he pacified the human and non-human forces that were obstructing the founding of *dharma* in Tibet. Secondly, he brought Buddhism in general and especially the transmission of the teachings and blessing powers of Tantra for his many Tibetan disciples and their followers. Thirdly, through his enlightened power he concealed numerous teachings and transmission as well as religious objects as Ter, for the benefit of the future followers, in the minds of his disciples.

While transmitting esoteric teachings to his realized disciples in Tibet, Guru Padmasambhava concealed (སྦས) many teachings with the blessings of his enlightened mind stream in the nature of the intrinsic awareness (རིག་པ) of the minds of his disciple through the power of "mind-mandate transmission (གཏད་རྒྱ)," and thereby the master and disciple became united as one in the teachings and realisation. Here, the master has insinuated and then concealed the teaching and blessings, the esoteric attainments, as Ter in the pure nature of mind of his disciples through his enlightened power and has made aspirations that the Ter may be discovered for the sake of beings when the appropriate time comes. By the power of this method, which is called the mind-mandate transmission, the actual discoveries of the teachings take place. The mind-mandate transmission is the heart core of the Ter tradition of Guru Padmasambhava.

Then in succeeding centuries, when the time for benefiting beings with a particular teaching arrived, the reincarnations of the realized disciple of Guru Padmasambhava discovered those teachings which had been transmitted and concealed in them by the master in their past lives, through the power of the enlightened aspirations of the master and disciples and the good *karma* beings. There are thousand of images, symbolic scripts, complete texts, medicinal material and ritual tools, etc., have been concealed by Guru Padmasambhava and discovered as Ter substances (གཏེར་རྫས), but the main Ter is the teachings and the blessings transmitted through the minds of the disciples.

Transmission of Ter

The transmission of Ter has been channelled through six kinds or lineages (བརྒྱུད་པ་དྲུག). Of the six lineages, three are identical to the lineage of general *tāntric* transmission in Nyingmapa scriptures. They are the lineage of transmission from, "enlightened mind to enlightened mind among the Buddha's (རྒྱལ་བ་དགོངས་བརྒྱུད)," the lineage of transmission through mere "indications among the knowledge-holders (རིག་འཛིན་བརྡ་བརྒྱུད), and the lineage of "oral transmission among ordinary beings (གང་ཟག་སྙན་བརྒྱུད)."

The next three lineages are unique to the Ter transmission and the accomplishment of Ter discoveries are based on those transmissions. The first is "the transmission of aspirational empowerment (སྨོན་ལམ་དབང་བསྐུར), or the mind-mandate transmission" whereby, through his concentration of enlightened power, Guru Padmasambhava transmits and conceals the esoteric attainments and the teachings in the field of intrinsic awareness, the enlightened nature of disciple's mind. This is the main aspect of transmission. The second is the "transmission through prophetic authorization (ལུང་བསྟན་བཀའ་བབས)," in which the master inspires the disciples and gives prophecies concerning his becoming a Terton in the future. It is not just a foretelling of the future; rather, by his enlightened power, he makes things happen that he prophesies. The third is "the entrustment to the *ḍākinīs* (མཁའ་འགྲོ་གཏད་རྒྱ)," in which the master entrusts the Ter, the Terton, the teachers and the followers of the traditions to the protection of the *ḍākinīs* and *dharma* protectors. In the case of Earth Ter, the master entrusts the objects, such as the caskets containing the yellow scrolls with symbolic scripts, to the *ḍākinīs* and *dharma* protectors to keep them and hand them over to the Terton when the time comes. Thus, every Ter teaching is transmitted through the six types of transmission.

Two Major Categories of Ter

While Ter is divided into eighteen categories and so on, there are two major categories of Ter based on their way of discovery. They are Earth Ter (ས་གཏེར) and Mind Ter (དགོངས་གཏེར). The discovery of Earth Ter involves earthly materials such as "symbolic scripts" (བརྡ་ཡིག) written on a scroll of paper known as a "yellow scroll" (ཤོག་སེར), and so on. These are to assist the discovery of the concealment or to awaken the memory of the Ter enshrined in the enlightenment nature of the mind of the Terton (གཏེར་སྟོན), the Ter Discoverer. However, people usually conceive that Mind Ter is transmitted through mind but that Earth Ter is something that Terton discover from earthly objects such as rocks, lakes, and so on. Actually, the symbolic script merely becomes the key, but is neither the real Ter of teachings nor the transmission of the attainment, which comes only from the Terton's mind.

Earth Ter (ས་གཏེར)

CONCEALMENT OF TER

There are different ways of concealing the Ters, but mostly they involve three stages. First, Guru Padmasambhava transmitted his esoteric teachings and attainments to his disciples and concealed them in their minds' absolute nature.

Ordinary mind is changing because of concepts and emotions, but the nature is changeless and preserves the teachings intact within it. The third Dodrupchen wrote:

> The ultimate place, the sacred treasure where the wisdom blessing of the Vajra-speech is preserved without deterioration through the power of the mind-mandate transmission made by Guru Rinpoche (Padmasambhava), is the sphere of changeless intrinsic nature of the mind of the Terton.[3]

Second, with his consort Yeshe Tshogyal, Guru Padmasambhava put the teachings into "symbolic of coded scripts" in various languages, mostly what is called *ḍākinī* language, and wrote them on "yellow scrolls," or on various objects such as images and ritual objects. Because of the power of the "aspirational transmission" of Guru Padmasambhava, the "symbolic script" will have the power to awaken the transmission when the Terton, the discoverer, reads it. Then the Terton puts the yellow scrolls in a casket and conceals the "casket (གཏེར་སྒྲོམ)" in a "place of Ter concealment (གཏེར་གནས)" such as rocks, mountains, lakes, temples, images and sky through his or her mystical power, and it becomes invisible until the time of discovery.

Third, Guru Padmasambhava inspires his disciples to be Tertons and gives prophetic blessings concerning when and how he or she will become a Terton. This is not a mere prediction of the future but a blessing which makes the prophesied events happen because of the truth of the master's word.

Discoverer of Terton

It is said that there will be one hundred major and a thousand minor Tertons. Starting from Sangye Lama (eleventh century), a great number of Tertons appeared in Tibet and thousand of volumes of teachings and a vast number of religious artefacts were discovered as Ter. Even today, since the beginning of

3. ལས་འཕྲོ་གཏེར་བརྒྱུད་ཀྱི་རྣམ་བཤད་ཉུང་གསལ་ངོ་མཚར་རྒྱ་མཚོ། by the third Dodrupchen Rinpoche, 4b/2.

twenty first century, the work of discoveries of Ter is going on in Tibet though the Chinese occupation had halted it in its earlier phase. Tertons are the reincarnations of the disciples of Guru Padmasambhava, and from him they have received the mind-mandate transmission of the teachings and have accomplished high attainments. With the exception of a few Tertons, most of them have been *tāntric*s living at home with families. They transmute their everyday life into the training of the union of bliss and emptiness without discrimination and propagate the teachings discovered by them. Some of the great Tertons are Nyag Nyina Odzer (1124-92), Guru Chowang (1212-70), Ogyen Lingpa (1323-), Rigdzin Doddem (1337-1408), and Sangye Lingpa (1340-96), Dorje Lingpa (1346), Ratna Lingpa (1403-78), Padma Lingpa (1450-), Tigdzin Jigmed Lingpa (1729-98), and Khyntse'I Wangpo (1820-92).

Most of the Terton, before discovering any Ter, seem to be ordinary people. They do not necessarily appear as scholars, mediators or Tulkus. However, due to their inner spiritual attainments and the transmissions they have received in their past lives, at the appropriate times, they suddenly start discovering mystical Ters without the need of any apparent training. At the beginning, sceptics raise doubts about discoveries of such unexpected people. In some cases, a Terton's natural directness and honesty may appear as unconventional or even impolite to those who hold conservative values. But gradually, if they are true Ter discoveries, they gain the recognition of higher spiritual authorities and establish the respect of ad (all) benefit for the people. It is important to understand this cultural context; otherwise, a great Terton might be mistaken for a charlatan. For example, it is unfortunate, that a Western author has recently in 1988 disclaimed one of the most authentic Tertons of the Nyingmapa tradition of Tibet by using some criticism made by unqualified contemporaries or made for ulterior motives, and the Terton's own expressions of humility, which are characteristics of Buddhist sages.

Discovery

The following is a description of the common process of Earth Ter discovery, but it is certainly not the only one, for Ters have been discovered in many other ways. First, the Terton receives the "prophetic guide (ཁ་བྱང་།)" in pure visions, directly or in indications from Guru Padmasambhava, *ḍākinī*s or deities. Then he or she performs "the Ter preparatory practices (གཏེར་སྒྲུབ།)", doing meditations or rituals as instructed in the prophetic guide.

When the time comes, The Terton goes to the concealment place, either alone or with the selected followers, such as his or her consort and heart disciples or just onlookers. Many Ter discoveries take place in secret (གསང་གཏེར།) and many in public (ཁྲོམ་གཏེར།). There, while performing "the feast offering ceremony (ཚོགས།)" the discovery takes place in different ways. It may be that the Ter descends from the concealment place into the hands of the Terton at the end of a rainbow beam, or the Terton climbs up the rock, which in ordinary circumstances is too steep to climb, opens a door in the rock and climbs down with the casket. Or that the Terton disappears and then reappears with the Ter, or the Terton uses a tool such as a chisel to dig into the rock, and after hard digging takes out the Ter or the Terton jumps into a lake and brings out the Ter; or sometimes the Terton discovers the Ter from images, temples and from the sky. Sometimes Terton discover Ters concealed at far distances through their meditative power, without needing to go there, for the Ter protectors bring the Ters to them.

Among the discovered Ter, there are also images, religious objects and ritual tools, but the important ones are the symbolic letters written on yellow scrolls. Most of the scrolls were kept in the sealed Ter caskets made of precious materials, stone, wood and so on.

Again, by the performances of more Ter preparatory practices, the Ter casket spontaneously opens and in it, the Terton discovers the yellow scroll. It is called "yellow scroll" because most of them are yellowish or golden colour, but in fact, they could be of any colour, length or design. In anyone of the yellow scrolls, the Terton may find the symbolic scripts in any of the various human and non-human scripts and languages such as those of India, Tibet and Ḍākinī Land.

The symbolic scripts are in various characters and they are categorized in three groups: Just visible (སྣང་ཙམ) is one syllable or more, but not necessarily a word. Just a basis (རྟེན་ཙམ) is a phrase or a few phrases, a sentence or a few sentences related to the teachings of the text, such as a brief outline of the text, a part of the text, the title of the text or an event linked to the concealment. Sometimes it is a piece of writing unrelated to the subject. Complete text (མཐར་ཆག) is a discovery of whole text.

The Terton sees, contemplates or unites his naked wisdom (which is), self-arisen from his innate luminous nature, with the symbolic scripts and thereby awakens the power of Guru Padmasambhava's *Vajra* speech wisdom, which is concealed in him. He decodes the words in the symbolic scripts (བརྡ་བཀོལ) and discovers the meaning, the Ter, from them. The discovery of Ter is the arising of the *dharma*-treasures of the ultimate sphere (ཆོས་དབྱིངས) as the power of the intrinsic awareness (རིག་རྩལ) or the arising of the power of intrinsic awareness as the teachings.[4] If you do not have the realization of intrinsic awareness of Dzogpa Chenpo, which pervades the ultimate sphere, you cannot discover a Ter or Guru Padmasambhava, which comes through mind-mandate transmission.

So, the symbolic scripts become the key to awaken the memories of the teachings and attainments from the expanse of intrinsic nature of the Terton's mind. Then after more than Ter preparatory practices, when the Terton sees the signs of appropriate time, he transcribes the teachings. Then, the Terton transmits the teachings to the followers and entrusts them to the chief recipient of the Ter who is called doctrine-

4. *Ibid.*, 30b/4.

holder (ཆོས་བདག). Doctrine holders are mostly people who also have received the transmission of the teaching from Guru Padmasambhava and have taken responsibility for the propagation of the teachings.

Mind Ter (དགོངས་གཏེར)

The methods of concealment, transmission and discovery are similar to those of Earth Ter. Except that they do not rely on any external earthy source, such as yellow scrolls as the key to discovery. In many instances of mind Ter, seeing or hearing symbolic words or sounds in visions causes the discovery of Ter, but usually the discovery does not rely on any external sources and there is no involvement of earthly objects as the means of discovering Ter. A Mind-Terton discovers the Ter by awakening the mind-mandated transmission spontaneously from the expanse of intrinsic awareness of his mind, when the circumstances have matured and the time has come.

There is a third category of discovered teachings known as Pure Vision (དག་སྣང་།). Pure vision teachings are not Terma. They are merely teachings given by Buddhas, deities and teachers in visions. For this discovery, the discoverer does not need to be such a highly realized person, and there is no mind-mandate transmission. However, there are cases in which Ter teachings have been discovered or designated as pure vision teachings, and when that is the case, they are in fact Ter teachings.

In the Nyingma literature, there are thousands of volumes of Ter texts discovered by hundreds of Tertons starting in the eleventh century and continuing to this day. The majority of texts concern *sādhanā*, ritual, prayer and various esoteric performances (ལས). There are a great number of texts on philosophy, meditations and the result of Buddhist practice in general and *tāntric* tradition in particular. Also, there are numerous texts on medicine, astrology, history and biography.

It is astonishing to realize the scope and impact of the spiritual treasures conferred by Guru Padmasambhava in order to improve the value of social, literary and spiritual life of Tibetan society and the offspring of its tradition, for over ten centuries without cessation. And it is shocking to see that even many Tibetans have little awareness of the significance of this tradition. According to Tibetan historians, Buddhism may have never been able to be established in Tibet without the blessings of Guru Padmasambhava. In Tibet there is hardly a single significant mountain, lake or valley which is not blessed by him individually by visiting, meditating, displaying miracles and concealing Ters in them. Even many physical marks such as imprints, spontaneously arisen images or caves of meditation are still visible. The Ter tradition includes some of the most striking evidence of the great imprint left in Tibet for the welfare of the world through the enlightened activities of Guru Padmasambhava. At the time of his departure from Tibet, he expressed his kindness and his promise to the Tibetans in the following words[5] :

> When you face the bad times of the Dark Age,
> Everyday and night I will come to Tibet.
> I will come to you riding the rays of the Sun, and
> On every 10th of the waxing moon, I will come to you in person.

Nyingma: Belief in Supernatural Powers

The *bodhisattva* Vajrapāṇi who is known as protector of the mystical doctrines (the Tantras) tells *bodhisattva* Subahi, in what way one can attain *siddhi* or supernatural power; which peculiarities one meets on the way to perfection; which signs usually announce the approaching of *siddhi*, and finally what it consists of.

In order to attain *siddhi* it is absolutely necessary to give up all forms of selfishness and to develop devotion, aspiration for *bodhi* and reverence for the triple gems. That ten vices have to be avoided, false stories to be the given up; the aspirant has to be good natured and full of energy and devoted to the

5. གསོལ་དེབས་ལེ་འུ་བདུན་མ་དེསཚོཁེརེད by Rigdzin Godden

religious exercises; he is not to lend his ears to heretics, demons, spirit, etc.

But first of all it is essential to take upon oneself the vows of moral conduct and then search for a *guru*. If the evil action of the present or past lives prove a hindrance in attaining supernatural power, it is necessary in that case, to build shrines, statues of Buddhas or *bodhisattva*s and the Yi-dams and to recite special *mantra*s, or one has to seek assistance for performing the *siddhi*-ritual. The assistance has to be of high order and the locality where the *siddhi*-ritual is to be performed must be selected very carefully. The best of localities or places are those which are hinted at by the *sūtra*s and which had been used by the Buddhas and *bodhisattva*s. In the absence of only places, it is good to go to a river or a mountain, so that no noises may disturb you. The surround-ing of the place must be quite and safe. The ground has to be dug up about one foot or one and half feet and cleansed from all rubbish, stones, bones, etc., then new Earth has to be put on the spot and upon this the hut should be built. In the hut there should be present tāntric figures, *maṇḍala*s, *yantra*s, etc., before performing a ritual the Lama has to shave and wash himself and to put on clean robes. Three times daily he has to perform the Tantra ritual of offerings.

The *dharaṇī*s consist of mainly of reading *gāthā*s and *mantra*s; a rosary of 108 beads (representing the 108 books of the *Kanjur*) is required and it is important to select the proper material for the rosary. Daily, the Lama should recite the special *mantra* of his Yi-dam, say up to several thousand times and at the same time he has to pay attention to the special *mudrā*s, in order not to allow the mind to go astray. If greed or anger becomes dominant, it is necessary in that case to meditate upon the 12 *nidāna*s (chain of inter-dependent origination). Of the good action must have to be directed towards the attainment of *bodhi* or supreme enlightenment, as all rivers strive towards the ocean. For the offerings, one should not use spoilt food or drinks.

Performing the ritual and reciting the *mantras*, one should hold a *vajra*, a diamond-sceptre in the right hand it is made of a special material according to the goal, which is kept in sight. The purpose of the *vajra* is to remove hindrances caused by the evil demons or evil spirits which are supposed to try to take possession of the body of the performer of the tāntric ritual in order to disturb his mind or to cause mental sickness, etc., and thus to hinder the happy end of the ritualistic exercises.

If the recitation of the *mantras*, the offering of *homa* (sacrifices) is not made according to rules and regulations; or if the practitioners is absent minded or speaks about worldly affairs, then Vināyakas (demons) will enter into him. As regards the recitation of the *mantras* and establishing the *maṇḍala*, nothing should be left out or be added. Everything has to be done according to the strict regulations. In order to attain *siddhi*, it is a postulate, that the performer is adorned with moral and other necessary prerequisites namely that he is industrious, neither jealous nor greedy, and that he pronounces the words of the *mantras* and *dharaṇīs* distinctly, neither too quick nor too slow; the voice should not be altered or lowered, it is not allowed to interrupt the reading and to fix the mind on other things.

If the Vināyakas penetrates into the tāntric-performer and also into the dreams of the tāntric, it is advisable in that case to consult an *ācārya* (*guru*) and to make a *maṇḍala* of five colours. It should be a large one, four feet from corner to corner and there should be four "gates." In the middle there should be an altar, beside it a seat for Vidyarja (*ācārya*). Further bread, perfumed water and filled vessels should be put up, and into them are to be placed different flowers and feathers of a peacock. The necks of these water-vessels (Bum-Pa in Tibetan) should be circled with a five-coloured thread. The *ācārya* first offers to the Guardian-Kings of the Tantras, flowers, perfumed smokes, food, etc., then follow offerings to the spirits and demons and the *dharaṇīs* are recited in order to drive the spirits and Vināyakas away. Such a *maṇḍala*-ritual is believed to ward off an evil action and to alter it into a good action.

For the performing of the *homa*-ceremony grains of wheat or sesame, mustard, lotus, etc., are required. Four to ten thousand of grains should be mingled with butter and put on specified wooden slabs. The oven in which the sacrifices are burned has a fourfold shape, the shape of a lotus, a triangle, a quadrant or that of a circle; everything depends on the aim of the sacrifice. In spite of fulfilling all conditions and removing of obstacles, *siddhi* is not attained, there must be some unknown reasons for it and then it is necessary to invoke day and night the Dhyānī-Buddha or tutelary deity, and most probably the deity will appear in a dream or vision and tell the tāntrica what the cause of the failure are and may also give advice as to how to remove those obstacles.

The approaching of the moment in which *siddhi* is attained, is announced by agreeable dreams, in which one sees himself sitting under a canopy or entering a beautiful place, climbing a tower or a mountain, riding on a lion, or on a white elephant, horse, etc. After such dreams it is adequate to strengthen the efforts and *bodhi* may be obtained within a month or a fortnight or even at once. If the attaining of *siddhi* is felt, a fast of two or three days is proper, besides this special offerings have to be made to the Buddhas, to the Diamond-ruler of the mysteries (Vajrapāṇi) and to the ruler of *dharaṇī*s. The feelings of loving kindness and compassions (*maitrī* and *karuṇā*) must penetrate the whole being, *sūtra*s should be read and a special *maṇḍala* built up as a protection. During other ceremonies, one has to observe whether the *homa* burns with small or big flames, whether it is causing smoke or only smouldering. The kind of *siddhi* which will be attained can be predicted by these signs or even whether one will reach or not, whether one will become honoured in the world or not, and so on. Other signs of attaining *siddhi*s are, the moving of the statue of the Buddha or Yi-dam in front of which the *homa* is offered, the face of the Buddha suddenly brightens by beams of light and a perfumed odour spreads all around and heavenly music can also be heard by those gifted with clairaudience. Verses with living flowers should be put up and mantras have to be recited with deep devotion and the desire for success has to be clearly pronounced in front of the Buddha or Yi-dam.

For a special kind of *siddhi* in the descending spirit called Patra-deva, either on the finger of the Lama or on a copper mirror or into the body of a boy or even into an object of worship. It is necessary to observe, most strictly, all the prescribed rules, and to recite or read the *dharaṇī*s a hundred or thousand times. On a lucky day of the waxing moon, an altar has again to be built up, as large as the skin of a cow; the spirit descends again, and most probably all worldly things and other-worldly things will reflect themselves in the mirror or on the surface of water (as on the *maṇḍala*). Offerings to the spirit are necessary and after this it may be that he discloses to the performer of the ceremony in a dream all his good and evil actions. If the spirit takes possessions of a boy's body then it speaks through him. It should however not be forgotten that in certain cases a demon, instead of a good spirit, may take possession of a human being; if this happens, it is required to act according to the usual regulation laid down for such cases, in order to drive the demon out.

The *bodhisattva* Vajrapāṇi, the Lord of Tantras said that some of the *bhikkhu*s (of the Hīnayāna) and others do not believe in the doctrine of the *dharaṇī*s and ascribe to them a demonical origin and Vajrapāṇi himself is considered by them to be a descendent of the *yakṣa*s. Vajrapāṇi however made it clear that even the Hīnayānists and Hindu use *dharaṇī*s. For instance, Maheśwar has said to have 100 *koṭi*s (class, kind) of *dharaṇī*s, Nārāyaṇa (Viṣṇu) has 30,000, and Mahābrahmā has 60,000. Surya (the sun god) has 60,000, Indra (rain god) 18,000 and every god has his special *mantra, mudrā*s and *dharaṇī*s.

There are eight kinds of *siddhi*s. They are: 1. Supernatural power, 2. A Long life 3. The medicine of longevity, 4. Discovery buried treasure, 5. The admission into the grotto of Indra, 6.

The art of making gold, 7. The transforming of earth into gold, and 8. The attaining of the precious jewel (चिन्तामणि).

These eight kinds of *siddhi*s are divided into three orders. The first, third and fifth are the highest; the eighth, fourth and seventh are intermediate; second and the sixth are the lowest *siddhi*s. All these *siddhi*s are attained according to the character and saintliness of the performer. By misusing one's power, it is for instance possible to submit on one's will even a *yakṣiṇī* (a female evil spirit, often very beautiful and tempting) which can give temporary pleasure and wealth, but will, in the end, try to destroy the *siddha*. Therefore such an invocation of a *yakṣiṇī* is most dangerous and should not be done by a true *tāntrica*.

The most exalted *siddhi* gives insight, invisibility, the ability to take different shapes and to conquer demons and evil influences of planetary constellations. The middle type gives, besides a long life, even worldly and spiritual wealth; reverence and fame, the lowest gives, by the power of the *dharaṇī*; superiority over gods, *yakṣa*s and power against the persecution by evil spirits and over poisonous and ferocious animals, etc. Attainment of any of these *siddhi*s is only a means to a more sublime goal, namely the attainment of *bodhi*, the highest enlightenment. It is however, believed by the adherents of the Tantras, that the way of devotion and the development of all powers latent in human beings, should be brought to the highest point possible. A true *siddha*, even if he has attained such supernatural powers as prescribed above will never make a public show of it, but only, if at all, demonstrate them to his nearest disciples. Supernatural power is, after attainment, abandoned and not used by the real *siddha*s, with some exception here and there. In all the *sūtra*s of both Mahāyāna and Hīnayāna, the Buddha and his foremost disciples are attributed with supernatural powers but Lord Buddha forbade his disciples to make a public show of it. He himself, however, in the early years of Buddhahood, demonstrated his supernatural power to the Śākyas and others in order to make them believe that he really had obtained Buddhahood. He may have done this reluctantly, when no other way of convincing them had helped.

Nine Vehicles of Nyingma

(༄༅།ཐེག་པ་དགུ།།)

There are said to be eighteen schools of Buddhism. It is so that some were divided according to the teachings, some according to the chief exponent available in the locality, some according to the practices, and some according to Tantra, etc. Broadly, there are four schools according to the teachings of Buddha. They are:

1. ***Vaibhāṣika*:** It is said that the followers of this school rely upon the commentary provided by the masters of Buddhist philosophy and their explanations of the sayings of Buddha. They are of the opinion that the words of Buddha carry very high meaning which only an enlightened mind can understand and not the common wisdom. Therefore they rely upon the explanation of the Buddhist masters of that time, hence got the name of the Group Vaibhāṣikas (Relying on Vibhāṣa=commentary).
2. ***Sautrāntika*:** On the contrary, there was volume of Buddhist wisdom that maintains the opinion that the teachings of Buddha are simple and self-explanatory. They should be followed by them-selves and there is always the possibility of the assimilation of the thought of Buddhist teachers in the sayings of Buddha. And according to them, any concoction of mundane wisdom reduces the effect and fruit of Buddha's teachings. So, for them, the sayings of Buddha are first and final truth. Therefore, relying of *sūtra* (words of Buddha) they have got the name Sautrāntika (one who opines that *sūtra* is the final). They rejected any explanation or commentary to the Sūtra.

3. **Yogācāra or Vijñānavāda:** They were also the followers of a different type who lay stress on the Yoga part of the Buddha's teachings. By the *yogic* practices, they claim higher goals and hence got the name Yogācāra (the practitioners of Yoga). Also, because they philosophically accept the mind as a receiver of all the teachings and hence mind stands transcendentally, so they got famous by their second name also, i.e., Vijñānavāda or the mind-only school.
4. **Mādhyamika or Śūnyavāda:** Finally, this group of followers maintain that all things are devoid of intrinsic nature baring none, got famous by the name Śūnyavāda. Also they became famous by their second name Mādhyamika for their achievements relevant to the teachings of middle way of Buddha, specially focused. Further the Mādhyamika also have two divisions, Svatantrika Mādhyamika and Prāsaṅgika Mādhyamika.

Of all the above four schools, the former two schools namely, Vaibhāṣika and Sautrāntika are considered in Tibetan Buddhism to be of the Lesser vehicle (Hīnayāna) and the latter two, Yogācāra and Mādhyamika are from Greater vehicle or Mahāyāna.

It will be noteworthy here that "all the sects of Tibetan Buddhism claim to hail from Mādhyamika School among the above four in teaching part of their philosophy."

There are four types of Tantra practices in Buddhism. They, as described by the scholars are: Kriyā Tantra, Caryā Tantra, Yoga Tantra and Anuttara Yoga Tantra. All the Tibetan Buddhist sects claim themselves to be of Anuttara Tantra.

The Nyingma School is famous for its system of "Nine Vehicles" or *yāna*s, which are the way to achieve emancipation or salvation (ཐར་པ།). As the Tantra is an essential part of Nyingma School, the nine vehicles are actually nine method of practising the Nyingma through Tantra. The tradition of nine vehicles in Nyingma is divided into three parts.

They are:

ཕྱི་ཀུན་བྱུང་དྲེན་པའི་ཐེག་པ། outer born vehicle

ནང་དཀའ་ཐུབ་རིག་བྱེད་ཀྱི་ཐེག་པ། inner born penance's vehicle

གསང་བ་དབང་བསྒྱུར་ཐབས་ཀྱི་ཐེག་པ། secret overpowering vehicle

All the above three vehicle are divided again into three vehicles each, hence completing the nine vehicles.

These nine vehicles, according to different scholars have different type of classification, but we will consider the classification which has the most numbers of followers and is satisfying and agreeable to the majority of Nyingma scholars.

The first one, outer born vehicle is categorised into following three:

(1) Śrāvakayāna or the Vehicle of hearer (novice) ones श्रावकयान,

(2) Pratyekabuddhayāna or the vehicle of solitary Realizers प्रत्येकबुद्धयान

(3) Bodhisattvayāna or the Vehicle of Bodhisattva. बोधिसत्वयान

1. In the hearer or novice's vehicle, the intrinsic nature of voidness of religion is not achieved, though the practitioner realises the intrinsic nature of the *pudgala*.[6] The Buddhist theory of momentariness is realized in its transcendental state. The fruits achieved in this path is that *sakradagāmī*, *anagāmī* and finally ***arhat*** (དགྲ་བཅོམ་པ།)

2. In the path of solitary realizers both the voidness of soul and voidness of *dharma* is realized and the momentariness is also realized in its transcendental state. The fruit of this path is that the practitioner achieved the status of *pratyekabuddhas*.

3. In the third path, i.e., *bodhisattva* path, voidness of all the *dharma* will be realised. The practitioner here

6. This term is being used by the Buddhist for soul. The Tibetan equivalent for it is གང་ཟག།.

follows all the ten *pāramitā*s and four conservations. The fruit of this path is Salvation.

The second *yāna* is inner born penance vehicle and it has fourfold practices.

1. In the stages of Kriyā Tantra the practitioner's initiation is done by water and *mukuṭa* (head throne). In this stage the practitioner concentrates upon the 'self' [བདག་གི་དེ་ཁོ་ན་ཉིད (*svatva*)] and gains knowledge of the fourfold voidness. The fruit gained in this stage is after seven Births. He gains the *trikula* Vajradhara ground.
2. Caryā Tantra: Here the person in addition to the above two initiations also gets the initiation of *vajra*-bell and name. The fruit achieved in this is after the five births, the four *kula* of Vajradhara ground.
3. In the third Yoga Tantra, all the initiation, viz., Water, throne, Bell, name and Vajrācārya is done. The fruit at this stage is after the three births the attainment of "one pointed ground."

The third and final *yāna* is of Secret *yāna* and it is also as its predecessors divided further into three *yāna*s as follow:

1. Mahāyoga,
2. Anuyoga, and
3. Atiyoga.

Among the above three, the *yāna* of *atiyoga* is same as the Right view of Tsongkhapa as it advocates the five paths and ten grounds as the method to achieve its goal.

Maṇḍala In Nyingma
(དཀྱིལ་འཁོར།)

Maṇḍala is a sacred circle, actually drawn on the ground or formed of grain, rice, gems, powder, etc., and used as a ceremonial offerings to deities; also an offering consisting of jewels, precious things, etc., placed on a circular tray and made to a deity, incarnate Lama or any holy personage. In every sect of Tibetan Buddhism the *maṇḍala* is found. Actually, *maṇḍala* is a drawing of the house of a deity and hence every deity has its own *maṇḍala*. So the GelugPas have the privilege of *kālacakra maṇḍala* which is essentially initiated by the Dalai Lama himself, other sects have innumerable *maṇḍala*s after each and every deity, in order to make the offerings. As an example, *maṇḍala* of Nyingma sect is cited and elaborated with the offerings.

Essentially, the mode of a Nyingma Lama's offerings spiritually to the *guru, deva, ḍākinī, Buddha* and *bodhisattva* is called *maṇḍala*. In the following lines, the detail of *maṇḍala* or the offering to the different deities will be explained.

Having wiped the *maṇḍala* tray with the right arm of sleeve, the Lamas take a fistful of rice in either hand, and sprinkle some on the tray, the foundation of the universe of mighty gold. Then set down the large ring, which is the iron griddle of the universe. Then in the middle set down a dole of rice as Ri-Rab (सुमेरु). Then in the order given in the attached diagram, are set down a few grains of rice representing the 38 component portions of the universe, each of which is named at the time of depositing its representative rice. The ritual for all sects of Lamas during this ceremony is practically the same.

During the ceremony it is specially insisted upon that the performer must mentally conceive that he is actually bestowing all the wealth of continents, gods and, etc., upon his lamaic duties who themselves are quite outside the system of the universe.

The lamas do the *maṇḍala* services in the following way:

Oṁ vajra bhūmi ah huṁ on the entirely clear foundation of Solid gold is *Oṁ vajra rekha-ah-huṁ*. On the middle of the outer iron wall is *huṁ* and the followings:

1. Ri-Rab, the "King of the Mountain"
2. On the East is Luiphegpa or *videha*
3. On the south is Jambuling or Jambūdvīpa
4. On the west is Balangchoi or the Godhanya

5. On the north is Damingen or Uttarakuru
6. On the either side of the eastern continent are Luiphagpo and
7. Luiphog
8. On either side of the southern continent are Nga Yab and
9. Ngayab-sen
10. On either side of the western continent are Yonten and
11. Jam Chog Gida
12. and 13. Either side of the Northern continent is Uttarakuru
14. There are mountains of jewels
15. Wish granting tree
16. Wish granting cow
17. Unploughed crops
18. The precious wheel
19. The precious Jewel
20. The precious Queen
21. The precious Minister
22. The precious Elephant
23. The precious Horse
24. The precious General
25. The Bumpa of the great treasure
26. The Goddesses Lāsyā
27. Mālā
28. Gītā
29. Nartakī
30. Puṣpā
31. Dhūpā

32. Dīpā
33. Gandhā
34. The Sun
35. The Moon
36. The Jewelled Umbrella
37. The Banner or Flag of victory
38. Which is entirely victorious from all direction and in the middle are the Gods
39. The most accomplished and wealthy of the beings.

I offer you all these constituent parts of the universe all complete! O! Noble, kind, the holy Lama, O Tutelary Yi-dam! Gods of the magic circle, and the collections of Buddhas and *bodhisattvas*! I beg to these all to receive these offerings for the benefit of the animal beings! I offer you O! Buddhas the four continents and Ri-Rab (Sumeru) adorned with the sun and moon on a condition of incense and flowers. Let all the animal beings enjoy happiness.

I offer, you O! You noble assemble of accomplished super beings of the outside, inside and hidden regions, the entire wealth and body of all these mythological regions. I beg you all to give us the best of all real gifts, and also the real gift of the mystic insight caught by Nyingma Lamas.

I offer up this fresh magic circle, through the virtue of which "Let no injury beset the part of purity, but let us have the grace of Jinas of the three times, present, past and future, and let us, the innumerable animal beings, be delivered from this illusive world."

I offer up solutions, offerings, confessions of sins, and repentance. What virtue has been accumulated by me and others let it go to the attainment of our greater end. इदं रत्नमंडलकामि निर्यल्तायानि।

The Universe According to Nyingma Lamas

The system of worlds forming one universe of which there

are many consist of a series of fabulous continents circularly disposed around the great central mass Mount Meru (རི་རབ།) that supports the heavens. Moreover, this is separated from the circle of continents by seven concentric oceans alternating with seven concentric whorls of golden mountains. The whole system is girdled externally by an iron wall, 312-1/2 miles high and 3,602,625 miles in circumference, which shuts in the light of the sun, moon and stars; outside the wall is perpetual darkness until another universe is reached. The primary support of each universe is a "wrap and woof" of blue air like crossed Dorjes (thunderbolts), upon which rests "the body of the waters" and in this latter ocean are set the "continents" with bases of "solid gold" and underneath the central Mount Meru are the hells.

The dimensions are as follows — Mount Meru towers 80,000 miles above the ocean, and it extends for the same distance below the waters. Enveloping it there is an enchanted ocean (རོལ་བའི་རྒྱ་མཚོ།) 80,000 miles in width and it in depth. To this succeeds a will of golden mountains named the Track of the neck-Yode, 40,000 miles high and the same in width, and beyond this an enchanted ocean of the same dimensions. External to these are consecutive circles of alternating pairs of golden mountains and enchanted oceans of gradually diminishing dimensions as to width, depth and height, viz., 20,000, 10,000, 5,000, 2,5000, 1,250 and 625 respectively, which brings us to the so called "continents" in the outer ocean.

The "continents" are really worlds, for under the heading of Jambūdvīpa (འཛམ་བུའི་གླིང་།) is included the whole known world, both oriental and accidental (all other continents specified by the Lamas are therefore purely fabulous, as a Hindu Mythology). The chief continents are four in number, one being situated exactly in each of the four directions, and each continent has a smaller satellite on either side, thus bringing the total up to twelve. The description of these continents briefly is;

On the east is "Lus-Phags" [(ལུས་འཕགས་གླིང་།) विदिः] or "the great body." This is shaped like the crescent moon, and is white in colour. It is 9,000 miles in diameter and the inhabitants are described as tranquil and mild, and of excellent conduct, and with face of same shape as the continent, i.e., crescent like the moon. On the south is Jambuling (जम्बूद्वीप) or our own world (sometime described as the Indian sub-continent by the western scholars which is a limited sense of it). It is shaped like the shoulder blades of a sheep and is blue in colour. It is the smallest of all being only 7,000 miles in diameter. There are found riches in plenty, but also acts of the same shape as the continent, i.e., sub-triangular. On the west, Balang-Che (བ་གླང་སྤྱོད།) or "the wealth of oxen" (गोधन्य) which in shape is like the sun and colour is red. It is 8,000 miles in diameter. Its inhabitants are extremely powerful, and (as the name literally means cow+ox+action). They are believed to be specially addicted to eating cattle, and their faces are round like the sun. On the north is "Da-mi-Nyan" उत्तर कुरु or elevated Kuru tribe (Tib. སྒྲ་མི་སྙན།). They are of square shape and green in colour, and the largest of all the continents being 10,000 miles in diameter. Its inhabitants are extremely fierce and noisy. They have "square faces like horses," and live on trees, which supply all their wants. They become tree spirits after their death; and these tree afterwards emit "Bad-sound" (this is evidently like many of other legends, due to a false interpretation of the etymology of the word).

The satellite continents resemble their parent one in shape and are half its size. The left satellite of Jambuling, viz., Ngayabling (ང་ཡབ་གླིང་།) is the fabulous country of the *rākṣasa*, to which Padmasambhava (པདྨ་འབྱུང་གནས) is believed to have gone and be still there reigning. And each of the latter presents towards Mount Meru one of the following objects respectively, viz., the Mountain of Jewels, The wish granting tree or the wish granting cow and the self sprung crops (མ་རྨོས་པའི་ལོ་ཏོག) . In the very centre of the system, "The King of Mountain, Mountain Ri-Rab" (རིའི་རྒྱལ་པོ་རི་རབ) towers erect like the handle of a hand millstone, and underneath it are the hells. It is composed of jewels; its eastern face is of silver, the south of jasper, the west of ruby, and the north of gold. It has four lower compartments before the heavens are reached. The lowest of these compartments is inhabited by the beings called (གནོད་ཡོན) usually interpreted as *yakṣa*, but really givers of injury and therefore bad genii — and these hold wooden plates. Above this situated the bead or wreath-holder regime PhrengKnog स्रग्तहर which seems to be abode (དྭག་པོ) of the *garuḍas*. Above this the region of the *nāgas*, above whom are "the eternally fuddled ones (ཏྭག་སྨྱོས།)" above whom the four great guardian kings of the Quarters (རྒྱལ་ཆེན་དེ་བཞི།.) And above Mount Meru, at an elevation of 160,000 miles from the base, are the heavens of the Gods, amongst the tower of which are the 33 sensuous heavens of Indra (རྒྱ་བྱིན།). Above Indra's and Māra's heavens of desire are the less sensuous heavens of Brahmā's paradise (ཚངས་བའི་དགའ་ཟུན།), PhulGa and JhanPhul Bang Byed (འཕུལ་དགའ་དང་གཞན་དབང་བྱེད།) and above all these is the god of Gods, The Primordial Buddha known as ཀུན་ཏུ་བཟང་པོ། (समन्तभद्र) is the highest *brahmaloka* called འོག་མིན། (अकनिष्ठ) which means The Supreme.

Inhabiting the air on the level with Indra's heaven is the circle of the eight Goddesses. These goddesses are:

1. Dalliance (लास्य) of white complexion holding a mirror in a coquettish attitude.
2. Garland (माला) of yellow colour, holding a rosary.
3. Gītā (गीता) of red colour, holding a lyre symbolizing music.
4. Dancing girl (नर्तकी) of green colour in a dancing attitude.
5. Flower (पुष्प) of white colour holding a flower.
6. Incense (धूप) of yellow colour, holding an incense vase.
7. Dīpa (दीप) of red colour holding a lamp.
8. Perfume (गन्ध) of green colour holding a shell vase of perfume.

Immediately outside these Goddesses, and also suspended in the air, in fix positions, are the seven precious things; (རིན་ཆེན་སྣ་བདུན།) of a Cakravartin Rājā or the Universal Monarch, viz.:

1. चक्ररत्न or the victorious wheel of a thousand spoke
2. मणिरत्न or the mother of jewels
3. स्त्रीरत्न or the jewel of a queen
4. महाजनरत्न or the jewel of a good minister
5. हस्तिरत्न or the jewel of white elephant
6. अश्वरत्न or the best horse jewel and,
7. सेनापतिरत्न or the jewel of a general.

The vase was for storing all the riches of the three worlds. In the inmost circle immediately around the Ri-Rab (རི་རབ) or Sumeru (सुमेरु) are:

ཉི་མ། Or, the Sun consisting of "Glazed-Fire" with its chariot drawn by horses and moon (ཟླ་བ།) composed of "Glazed-water" with its chariot and seven horses.

Also there is the jewelled umbrella of sovereignty (རིན་པོ་ཆེའི་དུག).

The victory Flag or (རྒྱལ་མཚན།)

And in the centre of all, in the heavens of Indra is the store of the entire treasure of the Gods.

5

Emergence of Schism in Buddhism

Origin of Schism

WHAT IS SCHISM?

Schism is an ism within the ism. There is a theory or system and if within that the development of another sub-system took place, which was not present before in that system, this incidence or happening will be called schism. The happening of this sectarian incident depend upon various factors. Usually it fulfils the changing needs of the compo-nents. In other words, it further conditions itself whether the need arises out of change of time, place or persons or the composite demand of all the three. Schism does not necessarily mean a division or rapture. It is also not a necessary rule for schism that the cause of introduction of this tendency is within the system itself only, it may be an external cause, too.

Why Schism?

Buddha, just before his *mahāparinirvāṇa* or passing away, occurred as his last discourse as follow:

> यो वो मया धम्मो च विनयो च देसितो, पञ्ञतो, सो वो ममच्चेन तुम्हाकं सत्था।
>
> After my passing away, the teachings of Vinaya, Dhamma and wisdom will be your teacher.

It was here only that the schism had started opening its wings. Just because of the teaching of the master is to be interpreted, and the master was no more for the direct interpretation or clarification of it, the difference of opinion arises and it goes on till the fragmentation. The factors which lead to origin of Schism are very much in built in any system, theory, philosophy or ism. We can say when an ism is founded, the founder is to see the present-day solution and to some extent he can also foresee the future problem and able to offer some solution for the practical approach towards its functions. But this solution itself has some limitations. One cannot predict exactly what will be the problem in far off future. Only the calculation is done regarding future and that will be based on the then situations. It is just as it could not be predicted before AD 1903 what will be the aviation problems and what will be their solutions? The great reformers, scientist and inventers have vision but they too are humans and they have their own limitation of subject, matter and time. This is also true in case of religious testaments and its functions. The very basic problems of the human life remains same, but its applications and utilities makes it more complex day by day, with the new inventions and the practical functioning of solutions becomes obsolete. This is so because they fulfil the requirements of the limited dimensions of time and space given by their inventors. It is needless to say that they too, like the physical machines need overhauling or upgrading. That happens like this: the garbage is thrown out and the pure updated system runs with the same basics but now with new applications — used to do this work of overhauling by founding new sects and subsects within the system or sometime going out of it. Life creates new questions everyday, we have to answer them accordingly, and not in the same pattern with the same ideas which has been already been said before.

Problems and Solutions

Just as life is a name of going on and the evolution process is unending. Buddhism advocates and practices the theory of momentary, but the branches of philosophy of spiritual enlistment that do not believe in evolution but advocated Big-Bang theory, have no answer to the simplest questions of life.

They protect themselves in the cover of the patent sentence, "Everything is in the hand of God and not in ours." Nevertheless, we are in the universe to do something and not just sit down with crossed fingers and let ourselves be mere spectators. So Fatalism ends and here only to start the theory of action and results and once it is in your life you will question every result or fruit for its cause of action.

Importance of Change and Momentariness

Our actions change day by day; and so do our problems. One is just finished and other is in the process of coming up. The role of religion is primarily to synchronize us with the life. Later on in the middle Ages, it became complex, as it had to deal with the social, political and other challenges too with the simple problems of religious nature. This is because the new religious systems have built home in this land and because they were from other civilizations, they too, have to modify themselves with the host religious system in order to become more acceptable. Buddhism too, has gone in various changes according to time and space with need of localization. This automatically created a Schism in the system. Though after some time, some vital reforms also took place in the religious system of Buddhism to make it more suitable to its habitants. Here the religion had made itself competent to what it is not meant for, i.e., the comparison and proof to be the better among the best.

In the sixth century BC, when Buddhism emerged out of the social system prevalent in the then societies of India, it was built to deal with every possible solution of the problems of the life. In fact, it starts with the encounter of Prince Siddhārtha with the basic problems of life, i.e., sickness, old age and death. The way Buddha found, was the eight-fold path, which leads to salvation.

Recitation of the Teaching

THE VOID

The passing of founder of a religious tradition often leaves a void in the community because there are no longer the possibilities of daily guidance and personal inspiration. According to Pāli sources, hearing the news of the *mahā-parinirvāṇa* of Lord Buddha, a monk named Subhadda who along with his troupe was on route to Vaiśālī became very happy. He did not hide his joy and started shouting that now he is free to do whatever his wish. The one, who used to say do this, do not do that is now no more.

After the death of Buddha in 483 BC it was felt by the senior spiritual leaders of Buddhism (Theras, etymologically the elder one) that a council must be called upon to recite the entire teachings of the master at one place and time to erode the misconception and contradictions aroused out of the absence of Lord Buddha.

FIRST BUDDHIST COUNCIL

Then the First Buddhist council was held at Rājgaha (modern Rājgīr in Bihar near the world famous Nālandā University). The venue was Saptaparṇī cave on the top of the hill Gṛdhakūṭa. History tells us that nearly five hundred *arhat*s were gathered reciting the teachings of Buddha to a definite shape of a canon. The only non-*arhat* at that time was Ānanda, who was the brother and personal attendant to Buddha. He was with the master with 25 long years without any single instance of exception and no one other than him was able to recite the words of Buddha. Tibetan Vinaya ("dul-b") says that just before the commencement of the council, Ānanda got the realization and the post of *arhat*, which was then made mandatory to attend in the proceeding of that council. The Mahākassapa sat on the seat of presiding authority and then begun the historic Buddhist council to recite and recollect the teachings of Buddha which was scattered in the 45 years of time span and also with different geographical boundaries. The teachings were put forth, one by one, by the Buddhist scholars according to their field of specializations. Upāli, who was specialised in Vinaya, recited the teachings pertaining to monastic disciplines. Once a discourse had been reported and corroborated, it was accepted as authoritative. Thus, council began the process of developing a Buddhist canon.

In an oral tradition, which India had in ancient time, people develop ability to memorize prodigious amounts of material, and although the *arhat*s had only heard Buddha give a particular sermon one time, they were able to remember it. According to A.K. Warder,

> Writing was generally confined to mundane matters such as politics and commerce, but religious teachings were memorised since this was assumed to be essential for understanding.

COLLECTION OF SUTTA PIṬAKA

The historical authenticity of first Buddhist council has been questioned by the modern scholars. They allege that it is the creation of Buddhist communities to authorise their canon to establish it in the pages of history. It is reported in Buddhist histories, which agree that the council resulted in compilation of Canon in five collections named Nikāya or Āgama:

1. *Dīgha Nikāya* : Consists of thirty-four long discourses of Buddha.
2. *Majjhima Nikāya* : One hundred and fifty discourses of intermediate length.
3. *Saṁyutta Nikāya* : The associated collection. Here the *sūtra*s are collected according to their subject-matter.
4. *Aṅguttara Nikāya* : It is the Enumerated collection in which the teachings arranged in accordance to the number of items discussed.
5. *Khuddaka Nikāya* : This includes small discourse and other short teachings, which were not included in above four categories.

As a whole, they called it *Sutta Piṭaka* or "The basket of the words of Buddha."

THE SECOND BUDDHIST COUNCIL

After about 100 or 110 years of the demise of Lord Buddha, the spark which the monk, who showed happiness over the Buddha's death, escalated into fire and there evolved sectarian tendencies in Buddhism. This time the monks from Vaiśālī were found violating the norms laid down by the Buddhist community. The Vaiśālian monks were covering these violations under new interpretation of the rules. The conflict started and gathered momentum between the Vaiśālian monks and other senior monks who were not in favour of any change and were following the rules of monks word by word. Whether these allegation of violations were true or not, or whether these violations were necessary adaptation of the Buddhism in the changed time, it is a matter of discussion. However, one thing is clear.

To resolve the conflict between the Vaiśālian monks and the other senior Theras who had put allegation on them, a Buddhist council was held in Vaiśālī. As Otto Franke wrote:

> It may now be considered as safely established that:
>
> (a) The books of canon as a whole are not authentic;
>
> (b) That the canon was not composed and compiled in one and same period of time, but that different books into being at different periods covering a considerable time;
>
> (c) That the contents of each books were not collected, but were composed, each by a separate hand, with more or less reference to pre-existing traditional materials; and
>
> (d) That even the first two *Piṭakas* (*Sutta* and *Vinaya*) can't possibly have been presented as finished before either the first of Second Council, even if this event took place at the intervals assigned to them.[1]

---

1. FrankeO, p. 2.

Nevertheless, the second Buddhist council saw great opposition within Buddhist order and the Vaiśālian monks were expelled from the order.

This event after the second Buddhist council called upon 100 or 110 years later the demise of Buddha, clearly stretch a line of demarcation which can be called the first Schism in the Buddhist order. Therefore, it is necessary to go in detail here, to know the proceedings of that event. Following are the ten rules which were said to be violated by the Vaiśālian monks. Under the rule of Kālāśoka the second Buddhist council was held at the place name Balukarama in Vaiśālī. Seven hundred monks participated in the proceedings under the presidency of Revat Thera. Nevertheless, The 10 rules[2] were:

1. ***Singalonakappo***: Store the salt in a horn for future use. This was against the 38th Pacitya rules of monks.
2. ***Dwoangulakappo***: Take the lunch after the shadow goes lengthier than two fingers distance.
3. ***Gamantarakappo***: Begging in the boundary of another village after begged in one village.
4. ***Awasakappo***: Holding the Upoṣatha ceremony separately in same area.
5. ***Anumatikappo***: Request for granting permission from the *ācārya* after the work getting done. This was against the rule laid down in *Mahāvagga*.
6. ***Achinnakappo***: The tendency to do the work on the pretext of done previously.
7. ***Amathitakappo***: Taking the milk that is in the process of becoming curd. This was against the 35th rule of Pācitya.
8. ***Jaloginapana***: Taking intoxicant drinks. This was against 51st rule of Pācitya.
9. ***Adasakanisidanakappo***: To use the seat that is not

2. The terms are given according to Pāli sources.

sewed by the linings. This was against the 91st Pacitya rules laid down for the monks.

10. ***Jataruparajataggahanakappo***: To accept gold and silver as donation. This was against the Nissagiya Pacitya rules.

However, the Vaiśālians were greater in number and had the larger number of followers too. Therefore, claiming that they are not violating but done the needful to the monastic rules, they organized a different council and they became famous under the group name Mahāsāṅghika.

Also, after the 235th year of the death of Buddha, the third Buddhist Council was called under the rule of great Indian king Aśoka. This council was presided over by Mogaliputtra Thera. This council was attended by 1000 monks. After this, when the sectarian tendencies within the system became more affluent and in the fourth Buddhist council which was held under the auspices of King Kaniṣka, the Buddhism formally divided into Mahāyāna and Hīnayāna.

Localization of a System

However, they distanced themselves from the orthodox group claiming that they alone are originally on the path shown by Buddha and the other group is going by the word only and not by the goals and aims of the teachings. On the other hand, the senior monks who were later on called Sthaviravādins (orthodox school of Buddhism) alleged that they are distorting the piousness and righteousness of the Buddhist followers and practicing the Buddhism according to their own whims to fulfil their mundane necessities, which was strictly against the spirit and teachings of Buddha.

This process of reinterpreting the teachings of the founder of a tradition is not, of course, unique to Buddhism: similar movements can be seen within Christian traditions, each of which tends to represent Jesus in its own image. Striking examples may be seen in portraits of Jesus: although he was born in Middle East, images of Jesus in North America generally look like the people who drew them and have no Semitic features, and it can also be seen in the Jesus picture in Chinese Christian churches that have Chinese features and a very Scandinavian looking Jesus in a Swedish Lutheran church. More importantly, each tradition tends to represent the life and teachings of its founder in ways that reflect its values, presuppositions and practices.

This is the story of every tradition in the same fashion. As in Indonesia, they believe that Lord Ram took birth in their country and the whole event of *Rāmāyaṇa* has occurred in their country. Their depictions of *Rāmāyaṇa* on the stages have local effects and their character of *Rāma*, etc., have the same physical typicality's which the Indonesians have. They have a small place named Sri Lanka too, which they called the place of Rāvaṇa.

Regarding the sculpture there are two broad divisions of Buddha's making of statue in the terms of Art that is, the Gāndhāra School and the Mathurā School. Gāndhāra School of art has its centre in Afghanistan and Mathurā School of art in present Mathurā. The Buddha's face in Gāndhāra art has mongoloid feature whereas in Mathurā Buddha's face is just like common people of that time in India. Likewise, innumerable examples can be cited bearing geographical and religious boundaries. The point to highlight here is that, time and place leave their marks on everything including system and the system persisting long, accommodates most.

Eventually, various school of Buddhism developed Canons, and surviving example of these indicate that there were significant differences between the schools (though they also accept many texts and doctrines in common).[3] One common pattern however was the collection of texts into three sections called *Tripiṭaka*s. However, this too is broken in Tibetan tradition and they shrink these three in to two divisions.

Thus, following the death of Buddha, the tradition which he had founded began to develop different factions within

3. Lamotte, pp. 517-49 and *Indian Buddhism* pp. 11-13.

itself, many of which compiled their own version of the canon, and each of which had its own understanding of the doctrines he propounded and the path of liberation that he revealed to his followers.

Theravādins and Mahāsāṅghikas

After second Buddhist council, there were two distinct groups of Buddhist in India. The Mahāsāṅghikas (the group of Vaiśālian monks and their supporters) and the Sthaviravādins, who were of the view that the teachings of Buddha must be followed strictly word by word without any further liberal interpretation; even they went saying to this extent that the word of master need not be simplified for interpretation, they are already in nature self-explanatory.

Mahāyāna and Hīnayāna

It took more than six and half centuries for Buddhism to divide formally into two clear distinctive groups. This time the venue was Pāṭaliputra and the king was Aśoka or Kālāśoka. The occasion was the Third Buddhist Council and the reasons were the same. This time, it was felt by every person concerned that during the long course of time, the necessary evils of any societies made their entrance in Buddhist assembly too. They started considering of cast, creed and other social prohibitions that were there prior to their entrance in Buddhism. They carried these values in the Buddhism too. In nutshell, in Buddhism there were the people who stood as Buddhists, which were free of class, social position, the supremacy of any kind and now, they develop these evils within themselves. The king himself was present outside the venue of the third council and with the help of the senior Theras, he purged those monks who were practising their own beliefs that are contrary to Vinaya Rules. After eliminating those people from the Buddhist order, the king forced him to return to the household life that they deserved. That time, the line between the orthodox and progressive became more illustrative. The division was a distinctive one until date. However, formally Buddhism divided during the great king Kaniṣka, when the task of writing the Tripiṭakas was also going on. The Buddhism divided into Mahāyāna (which was Mahāsāṅghika or the progressive group) and the Sthaviravāda (also called Hīnayāna by Mahāyānists). However, as time passed on, the difference domains broadened and now the difference can be seen in the terms of the countries.

Theravāda is predominant in South-East Asia. It is generally conservative tradition with its scriptures' base in Pāli canons, which can be traced back to historical Buddha. Mahāyāna, the other major tradition of Buddhism believes that the Pāli texts are only a portion of what the Buddha taught, and it emphasized other texts written in Buddhist hybrid Sanskrit (as termed by the linguistics). Theravāda rejected those texts as foreigners. Mahāyāna is predominant in East and Central Asia. India however, more or less came under the category of Hīnayāna or Sthaviravāda as they preferred to call themselves. Nevertheless, during past 30 to 40 years it welcomed Mahāyāna also. There are large Mahāyāna monasteries also with the traditional Hīnayāna Buddhist monasteries.

The credit of which is attributed not to the Indian Buddhists but to the Tibetan people and the temporal Head, His Holiness the XIV Dalai Lama of Tibet, Tenzin Gyatso who escaped to India in May 1959 in order to safeguard himself and Tibetan communities from Chinese authorities. The Dalai Lama along with 7900 monks and 800 Tulkus and several thousand common people of his country entered India as refuge and is since working dynamically to save his religious, cultural and social tradition. The three great monasteries were built in Karnataka near Mundgod with the cooperation of Indian government. The fourth great monastery, Tashilhunpo was also built in Uttar Pradesh.

However, Hīnayāna also continued to enjoy the native followers. The Baba Bhim Rao Ramji Ambedkar also contributed when he became instrumental to convert several thousand brow-beaten people at Nagpur in Maharashtra towards Buddhism in 1956.

The seed of Schism were sown even during the time of Buddha himself which ripened after the death of Buddha and further brought result finally during the period of Kaniṣka. Nowadays there are several groups and sub-groups, factions and semi-faction within the same sects. The basic tendency of individualism seems to carry the human towards the practicing the Schism.

6

Heritage of Tibetan Translated Literature

THE history of Tibetan translated literature has its beginning in the seventh century when the whole of the Tibet was brought under the rule of Song Tsan Gampo [(སྲོང་བཙན་སྒམ་པོ) born AD 617]. Although the Chief of a small principality, he mobilized a strong army and brought under his control both the U (དབུས) and Tsang (གཙང་།) provinces. His conquests extended up to Gilgit in the west and Chinese Turkistan in the north. The Chinese emperor and the Nepalese king had to part with certain territories of their dominations to the Tibetans. In recognition of his might and expanding power, both the Chinese and Nepalese kings consented to give their daughters in marriage to the Tibetan king.

Song-Tsan Gam-Po was not only a great conqueror and an able ruler but also a far-sighted and enlightened monarch. Until his reign, Tibet had been a country inhabited by wild and warlike people. They were believers of Bon, a cult that believed in the power of spirits. Civilization and a cultured way of life were yet to set in. Persuaded by his two queens, both of them were devout Buddhists, Song-Tsan Gam Po decided to introduce Buddhism into his country. A religious literature in the national language was considered essential, so if Buddha's doctrine was to set its feet firmly on Tibetan soil it had to be in the national language. The Tibetan language, however, was not suitably rendered into writing at that time. Song-Tsan therefore, deputed Thon-mi Sam Bho Ta, and India and intelligent Tibetan youth in the company of sixteen others, to proceed to India and study Sanskrit and Buddhist texts and to develop a script suitable for rendering the Buddhist texts in the native language.

Thon-mi, having arrived in AD 632 (according to traditional sources), studied in Nalanda University under two teachers, Deva Vidya Singh and Brahmin Lipikara. On the return to Tibet, the first thing he did was to design the Tibetan alphabets on the model of western Gupta script. Thon-Mi Sam Bho Ta (or "The good Tibetan"— a title given to him by the Indians) is accredited with the authorship of eight works on grammar, only two of which; Sum-Cu-Pa (གསུམ་བཅུ་པ།) and Tag-Jug-Pa (རྟགས་ཀྱི་འཇུག་པ།) are available today.

Thereafter, under the patronage of the king, Thon-mi began the translation of Sanskrit texts that he had brought from India, into the Tibetan language. He was helped in his work by the Indian Puṇḍit Kusar, the Nepalese Shila Manju, the Kashmiri Tun, the Chinese Bhikshu Mahadev and his own disciple, Choe Jod (ཆོས་མཛོད). Works such as *Karaṇḍavyūha Sūtra* (ཟ་མ་ཏོག་བཀོད་པའི་མདོ), a *sūtra* of aphorism on the good qualities of Avalokiteśvara taught by Śākyamuni to an audience of 1,250 priests at Śrāvastī, *Ratnamegh Sūtra* (དཀོན་ཆོག་སྤྲིན་གྱི་མདོ) and *Karma Śataka* (མཛད་བརྒྱ), were translated. Besides the scholars named, there were others from Chinese Turkistan who collaborated with Thonmi-Sam-Bho-Ta. The Chinese translators concentrated on astrology and medicine.

Between AD 730 and 802, according to Alexander Csoma de Koros, the *Suharna Prabasotam Sūtra* (གསེར་འོད་དམ་པ) was translated by Jina Mitra, Shila Indra Bodhi and Wendei Shede (ཞེན་དེ་ཡེ་ཤེས་སྡེ།). It contains several articles on both the dogmatism and moral doctrine of the Buddhist faith.

The great Indian Puṇḍit Śāntarakṣita visited Tibet during the reign of King Thi Song Deu-Tsen (ཁྲི་སྲོང་ལྡེའུ་བཙན AD 802-45) and laid the foundation of an organized monkhood in the snowy country. He also helped the Tibetans to build the monastery of Sam-Ye (བསམ་ཡས.). Apart from other engagements, Śāntarakṣita devoted enough time to translation works, which were part of the Indian missionary activities. With the help of *Dharma Kośa*, he translated the *Hetu Cakra* (རྒྱུའི་འཁོར་ལོ) of Dignāng. Another Indian *ācārya* to visit Tibet was Kamalaśīla. During this time the Indian *ācārya*s like Vimalmitra, Buddha Gupta, Śānti Garbha and Bishuda Sinha, in collaboration with Tibetan Lo Tsa Ba[1] (s) like *Dharmaloka*, Go Rinchen De (གོ་རིན་ཆེན་སྡེ) and Śākyaprabha, rendered several Buddhist texts into Tibetan. However, until the ascendancy of king Thi Song Deu Tsan [(ཁྲི་སྲོང་ལྡེའུ་བཙན་པོ) AD 847-77] to the Tibetan throne, the translation work could not serve the purpose for which it was intended. In other words, the translation was done in such a language that it was unintelligible to the common masses. In some cases, they were re-translated from the Chinese, which could not provide uniform word-to-word equivalents. Under the direction of the king, definite rules were laid down for the translation of Sanskrit originals into Tibetan, from the middle of the ninth century onwards; all translation works were undertaken in strict conformity to these rules. A *Sanskrit-Tibetan Dictionary Mahāvyutpatti* (ཛེ་དག་ཏུ་རྟོག་པར་ཛེ་པ་ཆེན་པོ), composed for this purpose, is still to be found in the Tan-Gyur (བསྟན་འགྱུར). The noted Tibetan Lo-Tsa Ba, Rin-Chen Zang-po (AD 957-1055) with the help of Puṇḍit Sradakavarma, Padmakar Gupta, Buddhaśrī Śānta, Buddha Pal and Kamal Gupta translated a number of philosophical and *tāntric* treatises. These included Haribhadra Abhisamaya Alaṅkāraloka (མངོན་པར་སྣང་པའི་རྒྱན), a discourse on right judgement or discernment, Nāgārjuna's *Vaidik Aṣṭāṅga Hṛdaya Saṁhitā* (ཡོན་ཏན་བདུན་ཡོངས་སུ་བརྗོད་པའི་གཏམ), a conversation or discourse on the seven accomplished good qualities, and *Sumag Avadāna* (མ་ག་དྷ་བཟང་མོའི་རྟོགས་པ་བརྗོད་པ) or the story of Sumagadha, the daughter of a rich and respectable householder at Śrāvastī in Kośala, who had endowed the Śākyas with a large religious establishment.

With the arrival of the great Indian saint Atīśa Dīpaṅkara Śrīgyāna, more works were rendered into Tibetan. Atīśa himself was a great translator. He translated the *Mādhyamika*

---

1. Tibetan term for a translator.

Ratnapradīpa (དབུ་མ་རིན་ཆེན་སྣང་བ), the work of the famous Indian philosopher Bāvaviveka, with the help of Rin-Chen Zang Po, and others. The *Kālacakra* (དུས་ཀྱི་འཁོར་ལོ།) *Jyotiṣī* was also translated during Atīśa's time. The doctrine of *Kālacakra* introduced the worship of Supreme deity under the designation of Ādi Buddha (ཐོག་མ་སངས་རྒྱས།)

The *Buddha Kapāla Tantra* (དཔལ་སངས་རྒྱས་ཐོག་པ), *mantra* addressed to Buddha Kapāla with directions on how to prepare a square *maṇḍala,* was translated by Sa-Kya Yeshe. Sa-Kya Yeshe or Gayādhara also translated *Vajra Dak Tantra* (རྡོ་རྗེ་མཁའ་འགྲོའི་རྒྱུད།) with the help of Go Khug Pa Lha Tsa (འགོས་ཁུག་པ་ལྷ་བཙས).

During the time of King Yeshe Od (ཡེ་ཤེས་འོད), the Tibetan Lotsa Ba Padma Ru Tsi invited two Indian *puṇḍits*, Smṛtijñāna and Vibhuti Chandra. They were among the few Indian *puṇḍits* who translated Sanskrit texts into Tibetan independently. Smṛtijñāna's own works *Catuspita Ṭīkā* and *Vācabmukha* were among the translations. *Nyāyabindu* (རིགས་པའི་ཐིག་པ།) a book on logic written by Dharmakīrti was translated by Ngon Lodan Sherab [(རྔོག་བློ་ལྡན་ཤེས་རབ།), 1059-1108].Yeshe Lo do (ཡེ་ཤེས་བློ་གྲོས) translated the famous *Mañjuśrīmūla Tantra* (འཇམ་དཔལ་རྩ་བའི་རྒྱུད།), a learned treatise often quoted in later Tibetan works; his assistant was Kumāra Kalaśa. The birth of another great Tibetan Lo Tsa Ba, Patsab Nyema da (པ་ཚབ་ཉི་མ་གྲགས།) correspond with the death of Rinchen zang Po (AD 1055). He translated the *Catuḥ Śataka* (དབུ་མ་བཞི་བརྒྱ་པ) of Āryadeva, *Mādhyamika Avatāra Bhāṣya* (དབུ་མ་འཇུག་པའི་འགྲེལ་བཤད), and introductory explanation on the Mādhyamika doctrine of Nāgārjuna, and Pūraṇa Bardan's *Lakṣaṇa Anusāriṇī* (མཚན་མ་རྗེས་སུ་འབྲང་བ), a commentary on *Abhidharma Kośa* (ཆོས་མངོན་པའི་མཛོད).

During the time when Śākya hierarch was in power in Tibet, Drakpa Gyal Tsan (གྲགས་པ་རྒྱལ་མཚན AD 1147-1216), a learned Tibetan scholar translated *Nyāya Praveśa*, a work on logic and *Caṇḍa Mahārośana Tantra* (དཔལ་གྱུམ་པོ་ཁྲོ་བོ་ཆེན་པོའི་རྒྱུད), containing among other topics discussions on the nature of the human body and the soul. The *Prajñā Pradīpa Mālā* (ཤེས་རབ་སྒྲོན་མའི་ཕྲེང་བ), a commentary to *Abhisamaya Alaṅkāra* (མངོན་པར་རྟོགས་པའི་རྒྱན), was translated in AD 1200.

Shangton Dorje Gyal Tsan (ཤངས་སྟོན་དོ་རྗེ་རྒྱལ་མཚན), with the help of Laxmikara, translated Daṇḍī's *Kāvya Darśana.* (ན་ངག་མེ་ལོང་།), a work on poetry, Harṣa's *Nāgānanda Nāṭaka* (ཀླུ་ཀུན་ཏུ་དགའ་བའི་ཟློས་གར), a Sanskrit drama and Kṣemendra's *bodhisattva Abhidharma Kalpalatā* (བྱང་ཆུབ་སེམས་པའི་རྟོགས་བརྗོད་དཔག་བསམ་འཁྲི་ཤིང་།), a political work on the deeds of Buddha.

The thirteenth century saw another great genius, Buton Rinchen Dub (བུ་སྟོན་རིན་ཆེན་གྲུབ), who translated the works of Durga Singh and Harṣa Kritti. His greatest contribution to the imported literature however was the review and rearrangement of the hitherto scattered translations into the two monumental Buddhist collections, the *Kanjur* (བཀའ་འགྱུར) and *Tanjur* (བསྟན་འགྱུར) and the preparation of an index for both.

The *Lokānanda Nāṭaka* of Candragomin and *Meghadūta* (སྤྲིན་གྱི་ཕོ་ཉ།) of Kālidāsa were translated some time in the fourteenth century. Puṇḍit Banaratna was the last Indian Buddhist monk who visited Tibet and continued the missionary work. He helped the Tibetan Lo-Tsa Wa in translating *tāntric* texts. From available records, it appears that the translation activity carried on until seventeenth century.

These translated works were the result of the intense missionary zeal of the Indians and the labour as well as ingenuity of the Tibetans themselves. It may be said that, in the history of translations, no such faithfulness to the word and spirit of the originals are to be found. These Tibetan works, owing to its purity and perfection, were further retranslated into Chinese, Manchu, Mongolian and other languages. By this process, the Tibetan language became the *lingua franca* of Central Asia and occupied the distinction that Latin once hold in Europe. Moreover, the translated literature preserved the manners, customs, opinions, knowledge, ignorance, superstitions, hopes and fears of a great part of Asia, especially that of India. The Sanskrit originals of these translations have been lost or destroved because of time and historical factors.

Perhaps some may be found in future in Nepal, Kashmir, Tibet and other parts of Central Asia. But there is no certainty they will ever be found. Students and scholars of Indology will benefit immensely if they go back to the Tibetan sources to find certain lost chapters in the history of India.

In the Twentieth Century

The work of translation of Tibetan texts into Sanskrit and European language saw its golden period in twentieth century. Though in Tibet much more work was not initiated by the scholars due to the fact that Tibet remained isolated in the international arena and it was very difficult to contact Tibet for an outsider. But as we say in English "Blessing in disguise," so it happend with Tibetan text when China occupied its area and the Tibetan along with their leader were forced to flee India. This opened them the opportunity to interact with the free, traditional *guru* India with the option of whole world, and thus paved the way of translating Tibetan texts into various languages.

Much of the works have been wonderfully done by the Central Institute of higher Tibetan Studies, Sārnāth; Vārāṇasī.[2] But prior to that, there were different centres in India which were either run or sponsored by the Tibetan Lamas or their European friends. In this connection, Kalimpong[3] and Kursiang, University of Calcutta[4] in the

2. Some of the few major works which have been restored and translated among others at CIHTS are as follow: (1) *Pratītyasamutpādasubhāṣhitahṛdayam* (2) *Ratnāvalī* of Nāgārjuna and several others.

3. Self teaching Reader for Tibetan and Indians named, "तिब्बती-हिन्दी स्वयं शिक्षक" by Geshe Tharchin is one of the important works published from Kalimpong in early 1960s.

4. Shes Rab Dong Bu is one of the few major contributions from Calcutta University Press. A.C. Banarjee and other have done tremendous job in 1970s. *Mahāvyutpatti* was also one of the most important book that was prepared as bi-lingual (Tibetan-Sanskrit) from here.

eastern part, Bylekuppe and Mundgod in Karnataka, Leh, Keylong[5] and Ladakh in the northern region have done remarkable job in translating and even creating new Tibetan text.

CIHTS continues his work and in early 1990s there was a Karmapa Institute opened in south Delhi and it is providing Geshe degree in Tibetan (Equivalent to PhD). In Dharamśālā, under the able guidance of his holiness the XIV Dalai lama, Tenzin Gyatso, the publication is going through at various levels. One of the major contributors in this field from Dharamśālā is Department of Information and International Relations (DIIR) which is providing not only the written, but came up with audio-visual programmes also. Rest all could not be continued or the personal aids were discouraged. However the Tibetan Studies in the various departments in Indian universities is going on and it will produce good results in the academic field of the Tibetan through the research and publication.

The foreigner especially American contributed a good amount of research work regarding restoration of the classic works in Tibetan and Sanskrit. Among others, I personally studied the *Hevajra-Tantra*, restored from Tibetan, transcribed into Roman and Sanskrit and translated in English by a US scholar Dr. L Snellgrove. Indeed this type of work is of an unmatched quality. Nowadays the Tibetan Books are being published from numerous publications outside India. The Snow Lion Publication, and Wisdom Publication have solely devoted themselves to the field of Tibetan Buddhism and they have come out with good research work production. In India the Library of Tibetan works and Archives situated at Dharamśālā in Himachal Pradesh, is fully devoted to the research,

5. A book on Tibetan grammar in Hindī named, "संभोट व्याकरण" by K. Angarup Lahuli reader in Tibetan in the department of Central Asian Studies, Panjab University, Chandigarh., proved to be very essential and was published for the students who wanted to learn Tibetan from Hindī medium.

publication and restoration of the Buddhist texts of Tibetan and Indian scholars, not only classical, but modern also. I myself on reading the Kaba Paltsang's book on the Tibetan terms which was prepared by LTWA in English, couldn't control the joy of seeing the brilliant quality of work.

Still more to go, the research work in the Tibetan studies needs to be strengthened so that the classic works in the Buddhism must be restored to its original, i.e., in Sanskrit. We came across many names of the books of Buddhism as reference in other classical works, but unfortunately they were either destroyed or we have lost them during the foreign rule in India. These books were preserved through centuries in Tibet. They can be restored, word by word as the Tibetan translations were found to be the closest possible translation of the Sanskrit classics. Works have been and being done, but we have miles to go, only the best of our efforts can help regain our own valuable material which is fortunately preserved in another tradition.

7

Gelugpa School of Buddhism

(༄༅། །ཙོང་ཁ་པ་དང་ཆོས་ལུགས་དགེ་ལུགས།)

TsongkhaPa

TSONGKHAPA, an important teacher from the Tsongkha region, from the eastern province of Tibet, was an excellent teacher and had spent many years travelling from one monastery to another in search of the various lineages of the Buddhist teachings. His studies and practices explored the full range of Hīnayāna, Mahāyāna and Vajrayāna doctrines as found in all the schools of Buddhism then extant in the land of snow mountains, studying with almost four dozen masters from all traditions of Tibetan Buddhism, the school of Buddhism established by him (Gelug) was in fact the first attempt at combining all Buddhist lineages in Tibet and the first appearance of what might be called, "first indigenous Tibetan Buddhism;" for the earlier tradition in existence at the time were mainly rooted in a specific Indian master, such as the Nyingma with Padmasambhava, the Kargyud with the masters TiloPa (Tillipada) and NaroPa and so forth, whereas TsongkhaPa's tradition was to represent a synthesis of the several dozen most important schools of early fourteenth century Tibetan Buddhism. The eighteen volumes of writings that had issued from his pen were to act as a major inspiration in Tibetan cultural history, ushering in a renaissance of religious prose and poetry. His efforts and inclination upon art, architecture and folk culture were expounded by his interest in various creating festivals such as the Great Prayer

Festival of Lhasa; and by the selection of specific artists and craftsmen he used in his building and restoration work as mentioned further in this chapter.

Birth and Early Life

TsongkhaPa, popularly known as Je Rinpoche among the Tibetans, was born in Tsongkha region (Tsongkha literary means "onion," perhaps this name of the region was due to the production of onions in that area in abundance) in Amdo province in the Eastern part of Tibet in AD 1357 (Bird year) and founded the GelugPa School of Tibetan Buddhism. He is one of the greatest figures in Tibetan history and is well-known and famous for his scholarly contribution, religious reforms, the missionary works in Tibet and above all, for the foundation for a new sect named Gelug (literary means the path of virtues) in Tibetan Buddhism. (The present His holiness XIVth Dalai Lama, Tenzin Gyatso belongs to this very sect.) As per Buddha's words given in *Ārya Mañjuśrīmūlakalpa*:

> You (TsongkhaPa) will do the works of Buddha after my passing away and fill the gap. For this that times a monastery in Snowy province (Tibet) will be named Tushita below.

In Tibetan:

ང་ ནི་ མྱ་ངན་ འདས་པའི་ ཚེ། ས་ ཡི་ སྙིང་ ་དི་ སྟོང་པ་ ན།

ཁྲོད་ ཉེད་བྲིས་པའི་གསུམ་ཀྱིས་ ནི། སངས་རྒྱས་ ་མཛད་པ་བྱེད་པར་འགྱུར།

དེ་ཚེ་ དགོན་ ཆེན་ ་རབ་དགའ་བ། ཁ་ བ་ ཅན་ ན་ ཡོད་པ་ཡིན།།

Similarly, we found other prophesies regarding the birth of TsongkhaPa from other sources also. His father's name was Lubum Ge (ཀླུ་འབུམ་དགེ) and mother was Shing Acho (ཤིང་ཨ་ཆོས།). TsongkhaPa was fourth among six siblings/children. According to traditional biographies, his birth was the culmination of a process of spiritual developments that began during a previous life, at the time of Śākyamuni Buddha. As a young boy he offered a crystal rosary to the Buddha, who presented him with a conch-shell and told his attendant Ānanda that in a future life the young boy would be born in Tibet, there he would establish a great monastery and become one of the most influential figure in the spread of Buddhism in the "land of snows." The Buddha then predicted that in his future life the young boy would be named Sumatikīrti (བློ་བཟང་གྲགས་པ།).

A further prophecy is attributed to Padmasambhava, who is said to have predicted the birth of a great Lama named Losang Drakpa. He said that Losang Drakpa would be born in Eastern part of Tibet, near China, that he would be considered an emanation of a *bodhicitta* (བྱང་ཆུབ་སེམས་པ།) and that he would attain the complete enjoyment body of Buddha.

Prior to the TsongkhaPa's birth, his future teacher, Kyabje Dondub Rinchen (སྐྱབས་རྗེ་དོན་གྲུབ་རིན་ཆེན།), had been in Lhasa and had learnt that on his return to Amdo, he would find a disciple an emanation of Mañjuśrī. After TsongkhaPa's birth, he sent his chief disciple to the parents with a protection knot, some relic pills and a letter of greeting.

At the age of three, TsongkhaPa took a layman's vows from the Fourth KarmaPa, Rolpay Dorje and received the name Kunga Nyingpo. Before taking novice vows, TsongkhaPa received many *tāntric* initiations and teachings including Heruka empowerment and was given the secret name of Donyo Dorje. When he was seven, he fulfilled his yearning to take the novice vows, receiving them from his teacher. It is here that he was given the name of Lobsang DrakPa, forty years later which was to become the most talked about and controversial nom de plume[1] in Central Tibet. At the following page, the Thanka painting of Tsongkha Pa, the founder of Gelug Order in Tibet is given. Below in the picture are the two chief disciples of Tsongkhapa; one of them later became the first Dalai posthumously.

1. French term meaning "Maiden name."

TsongkhaPa's eminent teacher took care of him until he went to central Tibet at the age of sixteen. Before the statue of Śākyamuni Buddha in the Lhasa temple, he offered prayers to enable his completion of all the stages of sutras and Tantra in order to mature and lead other trainees to enlightenment.

Travelling with Denma Rinchen Pa in autumn of the year of Bull (1357), TsongkhaPa arrived at Drigung, a five days journey[2] from Lhasa, where he met the head Lama of Drigung Kargyud monastery, Chenga Chokyi Gyalpo. This great Lama was his first teacher (of Kargyud sect of Buddhism in Tibet) after leaving his original master of Nyingma (Kyabje Dondub Rinchen) who tutored him on various topics such as *bodhicitta* and *mahāmudrā* during his stay at the monastery. He also met the great doctor Konchog Kyab who taught him the major medical treatises and by the time he was seventeen; he had become an excellent doctor.

TsongkhaPa received different teachings and initiations, read numerous Buddhist texts. If it were to be described according to the study, it alone will become a dissertation. But for the sake of my subject-matter and as per the need of my research, I have tried to summarize them as follow:

TsongkhaPa started his study when he was merely six years old. He then studied with Tashi Sengyi and DersPa in Chodra ChenPo monastery in Nyethang. Yonten Gyatso taught him the method of reading great treatises and also helped him with the "Ornament for the realization." Soon he mastered all the works of Maitreya Buddha. Then he gained the knowledge of Prajñāpārmitā at great speed and little effort. TsongkhaPa, when finished studying the perfection of wisdom books (Prajñāpārmitā), was recognized as a great scholar at

2. In the old days in Tibet, the distances were measured in days and people used to spend night in inns. Hence, remember the days they cover to complete the journey and that become the standard for the distance. This process was found in almost all the civilization including Indian. *Kathāsritsāgar* is full of such stories developed in the inns.

the young age of 19. Then TsongkhaPa started debating everywhere and with everyone whenever he found an opportunity. He debated in various monasteries and became very famous. He then visited the great Zhalu monastery in central Tibet and received Heruka initiation from the renowned scholar of that time Khenchen Rinchen Namgyal. Then from the Lama Denchog Maitri, he received the initiation of thirteen deities, Yamantaka Practice.

TsongkhaPa and Rendawa

Je TsongkhaPa continued with many other required debates on the systems of tenets and the five major treatises[3] at various monasteries. Among others, TsongkhaPa met Venerable Rendawa and they both developed very amicable relations with each other. TsongkhaPa, for the rest of his life regarded him as his principle teacher. But the relationship between them was so intense and reciprocal that they were each other's master and disciple. TsongkhaPa received many teachings including the teachings of middle way (Mādhyamika philosophy) from Rendawa. TsongkhaPa composed a verse in the honour of Rendawa and would often recite it:

> Manjuśrī, lord of stainless omniscience,
> Avalokiteśvara, mighty treasure of immaculate love,
> O Rendawa Zonnu Lodro,
> I make this request, crown jewel of Tibetan sages,
> Grant protection to me, a fly seeking liberation.

Rendawa replied that this was more applicable to TsongkhaPa than to him and so adapted the stanza as follows. This is now regarded as the TsongkhaPa *Mantra*:

> Avalokiteśvara, mighty treasure of immaculate love,
> Manjuśrī, lord of stainless knowledge,

---

3. These texts were: 1. *Mādhyamika Philosophy* (དབུ་མའི་གྲུབ་མཐའ།), 2. *Logic*, 3. *Knowledge* (རིག་པ།), 4. *Prajñāpāramita* (ཕར་ཕྱིན།) and, 5. *Vinaya* (འདུལ་བ།). Later on, these became an integral part of the syllabus of Geshe degree which is equivalent to PhD of modern education.

Vajrapāṇi, destroyer of all demonic forces,
O Je TsongkhaPa, Lobsang DrakPa,
Crown jewel of the sages of land of snow,
Humbly I request your blessing.

From Je Rendawa, TsongkhaPa received important among others the teaching and auto-commentary of Candrakīrti's *Entrance to the Middle way*. He received from Kazhiva Losal of Nyethang the root text of Vinaya and *The Treasury of Knowledge*.

By this time he had completed an effortless single-pointed concentration on insight meditation.

He gave his first teaching at Nyethang on Metaphysics (*Abhidharma*) and Asaṅga's *Compendium of Knowledge*. He received teachings on Dharmakīrti's commentary on *The Compendium of Valid Cognition*. While at Śākya with Rendawa, he received an explanation on the root Tantra of Hevajra from Dorje Rinchen. This lama also taught him a method by which to cure his back pain that was troubling TsongkhaPa since winter that year. People, family members and scholars from Tsongkha valley requested so many times to return home, but TsongkhaPa wanted to continue his study in the company of Je Rendawa. But he was also moved by the compassion, for his home. To balance this, instead of returning home, he sent his mother a letter containing self-portrait which spoke to her when she opened it. Actually, from the childhood, TsongkhaPa always possessed a strong sense of renunciation and later on even refused an invitation from the emperor of China, who had requested his services as imperial Tutor.

At Narthang,[4] where the Tibetan wooden blocks of *Kanjur* and *Tanjur* have been kept, he met the great translator, Danzang.

TsongkhaPa, used to be calm and straight, lived without affluence or great comfort but sometimes tempered short while engaged in scholarly debate.

4. Nowadays available *Kanjur* and *Tanjur* are of the very same, i.e., Narthang Blocks.

However, his studies went on and on swiftly and at the age of 21, he became full-fledged monk (དགེ་སློང་།). At Drigung, he acquired teaching in the six doctrined of Naropa and the works of Phagmo DrukPa (one of the foremost disciple of GampoPa, the founder of Kargyud sect), from the great Lama.

By this time, TsongkhaPa had received from his DrukPa Kargyud master all the teachings that the great MarPa had given to two of his sons: MilarePa and Ngogchu Dorje.

At the age of 32, he travelled to Tsay Gungthang where he commenced a commentary of the *Prajñāpārmitā sūtra*. He called his work as Legs Shes Ser Tsang (ལེགས་ཤེས་གསེར་གཙང་།) or *The Golden Rosary of Eloquent teaching*.

TsongkhaPa returned to Nyethang and studied Kālacakra cycle and received relevant teachings from Thubten Yeshe Gyaltsen, who lived near Lhasa. This teacher also imparted the relevant instruction on astrology and *maṇḍala* construction. TsongkhaPa took Sarasvatī, a deity of wisdom as his particular protector deity.

While studying at Monkar Tashi Dong, south of Lhasa, TsongkhaPa was requested to teach in the tradition of Geshe ShatonPa and others of that lineage who had dealt with as many as eleven volumes during the period of their one teaching. TsongkhaPa agreed to do so after a 20 days retreat to prepare himself for that. Finally, from the 24th day he started his teaching and handled not merely 11, but 17 texts in 3 months during his schedule. Each day was divided into 15 sessions between dawn and dusk and the texts covered were as follow:

1. Commentary on the *Compendium of Valid Cognition.*
2. *Ornament for the Realizations.*
3. *Treasury of knowledge.*
4. *Compendium of Knowledge.*
5. *Sūtra of Vinaya.*
6. The latter four works of Maitreya.

7. The five texts by Nāgārjuna.
8. *Entrance to the Middle Way.*
9. Āryadeva's Four hundred verses.
10. Śāntideva's *A Guide to the Bodhisattva Ways of Life.*

After that, TsongkhaPa wanted to concentrate on the four classes of Tantra. On his way he met once again Rendawa at a place Tagten and received the *Guhyasamāja Tantra*. Rendawa advised him too to concentrate on *Tripiṭaka* (*Vinaya, Sutta* and *Abhidhamma*)

TsongkhaPa returned to Lama UmaPa Pawo Dorje who gave him external, internal and secret Kālacakra teaching. At that time the living tradition of Kālacakra was in danger of extinction.

TsongkhaPa went to Zhalu once again and received three lower classes of Tantra from the Nyingma lama Kyung Po LhayPa. He also received the teachings of the tradition of *mahāsiddhas* Lauhapāda, Ghaṇṭapāda and Kṛṣṇapāda.

After visiting Buddha Śākyamuni Temple during the festival Gawa Dong, TsongkhaPa went in retreat and received many *tāntric* lineages, teachings and initiations including Mañjuśrī Dharmacakra. Henceforth Mañjuśrī and TsongkhaPa became teacher and disciple. From this time onward Je Rinpoche was able to question *bodhisattva* Mañjuśrī on any topic at any time.

Then TsongkhaPa, on advice of Mañjuśrī took eight disciples and went into retreat for four years.

The Lam-Rim Teachings

TsongkhaPa took the restoration of the temple of Maitreya and it was considered one of his major works. He wrote two prayers composed and given to him by Mañjuśrī; a praise of Maitreya and a prayer for rebirth in the pure realm of *Sukhāvatī.*

The Nyingma lama Lhodrog Khenchen Namkha Gyaltsen invited TsongkhaPa to his residence at the Lhodro

Drawo Monastery to answer some questions. When they met, the lama saw him as Mañjuśrī and TsongkhaPa saw him as Vajrapāṇi. TsongkhaPa then requested the Lama to give teachings on Guru-yoga. Khenchen agreed happily to do so.

The oral teachings of KadamPa tradition coming from Atīśa had been passed to Atīśa's chief disciple, the layman Dromtonpā. He in turn passed on the lineage in three distinct lines. The "Textual Kadam lineage" was given to Geshe Potona and emphasized the need for a thorough comprehension of the meaning of Buddha's actual words entirely, not omitting even a single word or syllable. The Kadam "Lam-Rim lineage" was given to GampoPa and places reliance on Atīśa's *Light on the Path to enlightenment*. "The Guideline instruction lineage" was given to Geshe Chen Ngawa, the disciple of Geshe Sharawa and depends upon the transmission of oral instructions, especially those Atīśa obtained from Guru Suvarṇadvīpa. This included the lineage of Śāntideva's *A Guide to the Bodhisattva's way of life,* in order to receive this, Atīśa had travelled to an island near Java.

Only the latter two lineages were taught to TsongkhaPa by his Nyingma master, for he had already received the first one earlier. TsongkhaPa and Khenchen gave each other reciprocal teachings, and this kind of mutual teacher-disciple association quickly became the pattern in TsongkhaPa relationship with his various masters.

At this time TsongkhaPa decided to go India for further instruction from the Nāgabodhi and Mahāsiddha MaitriPa. But for the benefit of sentient beings, he remained in Tibet. Also, the hot and humid climate of India was considered unbearable for him.

At this point, I want to mention the view of Kyabje Trijang Rinpoche, (*guru* in the lineage of Phabongkha Rinpoche; he was the teacher of my Tibetan teacher Geshe Gelek Gyatso) the junior tutor of present Dalai Lama (died in India in 1983). He said once that if TsongkhaPa would have finally decided to come to India; we may not have had his greatest of great treatise named Lam-Rim (Great Exposition of the graded path to enlightenment). So it was better that TsongkhaPa remained in Tibet instead of coming to India. TsongkhaPa stayed at Narthang studying Lam-Rim by Geshe Thrinlay.[5]

Je Rinpoche then travelled south to Lhasa and there he met Gyaltsab Dharma Rinchen of Śākya tradition. At first the Śākya master didn't recognize and accepted the mastery of TsongkhaPa, but when he himself participated in a discourse given by TsongkhaPa, he prostrated to Je Rinpoche and became one of the former disciple of TsongkhaPa.

TsongkhaPa returned to Wolka chug for a year long retreat. During the retreat, he realized the vision of Nāgārjuna (ཀླུ་སྒྲུབ།) with his disciples. Then he gained non-conceptual understanding of emptiness. He then composed a text in the praise of Buddha's interrelationship of all phenomena. This text, popularly called *Essence of Eloquent* and also the text *In the praise of Relativity* mention how he was unable to restrain his tears whenever he thought of the Buddha's kindness in teaching the *Perfection of the wisdom* at vulture peak at Rājgṛha.

TsongkhaPa then reached Reting monastery (founded by Dromtonpa) with Rendawa. Here in Reting, TsongkhaPa wrote, *Great Exposition of the Stages of Path,* the ever greatest work considered in Tibetan Buddhism not only by the Gelug, but by the followers of other sub sects as Śākya, Kargyud and the former Nyingma.

When TsongkhaPa was forty, Yonten Gyatso invited him along with Rendawa, Nantse Deng and others. They all spent

---

5. Some of the Gelug scholars are of the view that the Lam-Rim teachings were not the original creation of TsongkhaPa but they were exposed by Buddha himself. TsongkhaPa was only to propagate them and throw light on them. However, this is not an acceptable view because all other historical, traditional sources prove that the Lam-Rim teaching started with TsongkhaPa.

their rainy season in retreat with the host as a sponsor.[6] Here TsongkhaPa gave elaborate discourse on "Vinaya" so lucidly that it is regarded as the second of his four greatest deeds. He also gave teachings on pramāṇa and "the middle way."

TsongkhaPa and Tantra

TsongkhaPa, on his return to Reting monastery, wrote a commentary to the *Fifty stanzas on the Master* to reinforce the paramount of such devotion in the Tantric vehicle.

Following many requests, TsongkhaPa wrote the *Great Exposition of Secret mantra* (སྔགས་རིམ་ཆེན་པོ།), the sequel of his previous Great Exposition, dealing with the path from the point where the previous text finished up to resultant enlightenment.

Nāgārjuna's *Mūlamādhyamikakārikā* is very difficult to understand and TsongkhaPa, at almost fifty years old was requested to write a commentary to it which he did. It is this time, when the letter from the emperor of China reached to TsongkhaPa requesting him to visit China and join there as a Royal tutor. TsongkhaPa turned down that offer on the pretext of his old age.

On leaving Choding, he asked two of his disciples about his wish to inaugurate the Great prayer Festival (Monlam) at Lhasa. He also ordered to prepare offerings for the same. In 1409, at the age of 52, TsongkhaPa assembled with 8000 monks in Lhasa and presented a crown of fine gold to the statue of Śākyamuni Buddha, which he consecrated, thus fulfilling the Buddha's prophecy.[7] This was the third of his four major deeds.

---

6. Since the majority of the Tibetan people were monks and according to Vinaya, they have to spend the whole rainy season without any movement, the food and other requirements were to be sponsored by someone so that the monk should spend their time not acquiring them, but in study and meditation. This remembers the situation in India where the sages were provided food and other mundane necessities by the common folk.

At the close of the great prayer festival called "Monlam" (སྨོན་ལམ།), his disciples concluded that now it would be unwise for him to continue his peripatetic life style. Hence, they offered to build him a monastery wherever he chose. TsongkhaPa, after receiving guidance from the deities in his dreams, decided to build a monastery at Drogri Mountain. This site was also mentioned in the prophecy of the Buddha. The monastery was constructed and it was named Ganden (དགའ་ལྡན།), the Tibetan equivalent name of Tuṣita — the abode of Maitreya Buddha. TsongkhaPa went to the site with one of his disciple Gendre Drub, later posthumously recognized first Dalai Lama. The Ganden Monastery was built as per Vinaya rules.

The following figure shows a *maṇḍala* different from that of Nyingma order. As I said a *maṇḍala* is a house of a deity where his offerings are made. The following *maṇḍala* is of Kālacakra which is the special privilege of Dalai Lama the XIV only to initiate. Hence *maṇḍala* is of various types and in all the sects of Buddhism in Tibet.

In AD 1410, TsongkhaPa gave his first series of discourses on Lam-Rim teachings in Ganden — on the *Guhyasamāja Tantra* and on Asaṅga's *Compendium of knowledge*.

In the 58th year of his age he composed a commentary on *Lauhapāda*'s *Cakrasaṁvara* (*Hevajra Tantra*).

TsongkhaPa decided to make a statue of Buddha Śākyamuni at Ganden. The consecration ceremonies were preformed; the Ganden main hall and construction of various figures contained in it were completed.

This is held to be the fourth of Tsongkhapa's major deeds.

In the year 1418 at the age of 61, he gave extensive discourses and wrote a commentary on, *A Guide to the Entrance of Middle way*. His complete works fill eighteen volumes.

---

7. See first page of this chapter; the prophesies for the birth of TsongkhaPa.

At the age of 62, in the year of hog, TsongkhaPa left his mortal body in lotus posture at Ganden monastery. Je TsongkhaPa, who was only 62 when he passed away to the heavenly abode, taught and achieved very much during his lifetime itself. This is especially true considering the much longer lives of Asaṅga and Nāgārjuna.

Even after his death, TsongkhaPa kept on directing his disciples by appearing in their vision. Khedrubje, one of his two disciples when encountered trouble explaining TsongkhaPa's texts, visualized his master many a times.

It is accepted among the scholars and communities of Tibet that the *Three Great Contributors* in the annals of the country were: Guru Rinpoche Padmasambhava (ཀུ་རུ་རིན་པོ་ཆེ་པདམ་འབྱུང་གནས།), Atīśa Dīpaṅkara Śrījñāna (ཨ་ཏི་ཤ་མར་མེ་མཛད།) and TsongkhaPa (ཙོང་ཁ་པ།), all of whom appeared when a great teacher was needed.[8]

Kadam and Gelug Tradition

This school of Tibetan Buddhism evolved as an independent school towards the end of the fourteenth century. Gelug

---

8. It was the 37th king of Tibet Khri Song DeTsen, who first invited the *bodhisattva* Śāntarakṣita to Tibet. At that time, there were many evil forces in Tibet strongly resenting the appearance of the Buddha's doctrine there, thus hindrances and calamities occurred. Śāntarakṣita advised king to invite Padmasambhava, who came and subdued these malignant forces, and then instigated the construction of the first monastery in Samye, south of Lhasa. After the repression of the Doctrine by King Lang Dharma, there was a period in Tibet when a very degenerate form of religion was practised. During this time, no one could find compatibility between the systems of sutra and Tantra, which were considered to be an irreconcilable dichotomy. It was Atīśa who dispelled such views and started the Kadam tradition. Later on, when people could not see how learning and yogic practice were to be united, TsongkhaPa came and revealed the correct path, established the Ganden monastery and started the Gelugpa sect, which has the largest number of followers with comparison

tradition of Buddhism in Tibet; or the path of virtue as it can be said in English, was founded by TsongkhaPa (AD 1357-1419), popularly known as Je Rinpoche, was a great admirer of Kadam tradition of the celebrated eleventh-century Indian master Atīśa and his chief Tibetan disciple, DromtonPa. TsongkhaPa was particularly attracted by Kadam's emphasis on the Mahāyāna principles of Universal compassion and *bodhicitta*; valuing these qualities not only as a spiritual orientation, but more importantly, as a way of life. In this regard, TsongkhaPa saw the study and practice of such Indian classics as Bodhicaryāvatāra of Śāntideva and the *Rājapṛkathā-ratnamālā* of Nāgārjuna as highly supportive to an individual path to Buddhahood.

However in TsongkhaPa tradition, the Kadam approach is combined with a strong emphasis on the cultivation of in depth insight into a system of learning and contemplation; the need to base the above two elements of renunciation. He called these three elements, Renunciation, the altruistic state of mind (popularly known as *bodhicitta* in the Buddhist world) and the Right View, the three-principle aspects of the path. In TsongkhaPa's view, a sound foundation based on these three-principle is essential for a successful practice of Vajrayāna Buddhism. It is a result of this emphasis that the Gelug tradition is said to represent a genuine union of Sūtra and Tantra.

TsongkhaPa's written heritage as discussed in the previous chapter is enshrined in his collected works, which run into eighteen volumes thus covering an enormously wide spectrum of learning and meditative practices, ranging from explication of the most profound aspects of highest Yoga Tantra, and the Mādhyamika philosophy of emptiness to the minute enumeration and analysis of the rules and precepts of a fully ordained monk.

In terms of meditative traditions, TsongkhaPa became the master holder of the three main classical lineages of the Mahāyāna Buddhist path. He inherited the lineage of rGya

Chen sPyod rGyud [The Vast practice (རྒྱ་ཆེན་སྤྱོད་བརྒྱུད།)], stemming from the Buddha Śākyamuni through to Maitreya, the lineage of ZabMo lTa rGyud [The profound view (ཟབ་མོ་ལྟ་རྒྱུད།)], which came from the Buddha Śākyamuni through Mañjuśrī and on to Nāgārjuna; and also the master of Nyams Len Byin rLabs rGyud [The inspirational lineage of realization (ཉམས་ལེན་བྱིན་རླབས་རྒྱུད)] which came from Vajradhara through the various lineage of *tāntric* practices. Through Lama TsongkhaPa these three lineages merged into a single major lineage. Additionally, in Gelug there is also several important transmissions known as Dag Nga (the close lineage of pure vision). Teachings belonging to this category are based on profound mystical experiences of highly realised meditation masters.

After a long, devoted and inspired spiritual training, studying with many of the great masters of his time,[9] TsongkhaPa established Ganden monastery in AD 1409. Ganden very quickly became a foremost centre of Buddhist philosophical studies attracting students and scholars from all parts of the Tibet. The followers of TsongkhaPa who gathered at Ganden (also known as Genden), later came to be known as Gelugpa, those from the Ganden school.

The spearhead of the Gelug approach to Buddhism: learning as much as possible, but doing so in the terms of one's own personal practice. The Gelug tradition has been condemned by some Western scholars as being overly intellectual. Rather, it would be more accurate to say that the Gelugpas make maximum use of intellect. Although their intellectual discipline is extremely vigorous — top scholars may study twenty hours a day for forty years — this discipline is never allowed to deviate from actual practice. TsongkhaPa dedicated many pages in the opening section of his great work "Lam Rim Chen Mo" to this theme. In fact, taking all teaching

---

9. Details regarding the Tsongkhapa's study with various renowned teachers are given in the previous pages of this chapter.

as personal advice is one of the four great qualifications of TsongkhaPa's lineage.[10]

Conclusion

Perhaps TsongkhaPa's greatest contribution to Tibetan Buddhism was his emphasis on using the three higher trainings — the essence of Hīnayāna as bases and supplements to *tāntric* practice. Of course these three were known in Tibet before TsongkhaPa's time but only in words. Therefore, the great translator Taktsang Lotsawa wrote, "some, clinging to the Hīnayāna doctrine, abandoned the Tantra. Others loving to *tāntric* system, disparaged the Hīnayāna. But you, TsongkhaPa, are the sage who saw how to put every teaching given by Buddha perfectly into practice.[11] Taktsang Lotsawa continues,

> You (TsongkhaPa) practised all Sūtra and Tantra, but specialized in Vajrayāna, you practised all Tāntric system, but specialized in Highest Tantra, you practised all stages of highest Tantra, but placed special emphasis upon the peerless illusory body yoga. O TsongkhaPa, unmatched treasury of teachings, I bow to you.

The higher training in ethics, meditation and wisdom was perhaps TsongkhaPa's greatest contribution to Tibetan Buddhism.

During the time of TsongkhaPa himself, many were mistaking emptiness, or *śūnyatā*, for a type of vacuum like object somewhat similar to that experienced by gods or the formless realms. TsongkhaPa asserted that such emptiness was not real thought of Buddha, Nāgārjuna, Āryadeva or Candrakīrti and that the liberation achieved by cognizing it was a short-lived freedom. In his opinion, the emptiness is best described in the theory of the absence of intrinsic nature in things.

---

10. Mullin.

11. Thubten, p. 618.

Among TsongkhaPa foremost disciples was Gyaltsab Je (AD 1364-1431), Khedrub Gelek Pelsang (1385-1438) and Gene Drub, later on known, posthumously, as First Dalai Lama. Following the establishment of Gaden monastery, many other monastic institutions were founded by his principle disciples; Jamyang Dorje Tashi Palden (1379-1449) founded Drepung monastery, reputed to be the largest monastery in the world before 1959. Jamchen Choje Shakya Yeshe (1354-1435) establish Sera monastery. The first Dalai Lama founded Tashi-LhunPo monastery in Tsang province which later became the official seat of Panchen Lama.

Subsequent generations also saw great luminaries who contributed to the flourishing of lama TsongkhaPa's tradition. These include such masters as the successive Dalai Lamas and Panchen Lamas, Kachen Yeshe Gyaltsen (1713-30), Gunthang TenPai Donme (1762-1823), Ngulchu Dharma Bhadra (1772-1851), and more recently the great Phabongkha Dechen NyingPo, popularly known as Phabongkha Rinpoche.[12] It is through the establishment of the major monastic universities, and also through the noble contribution of these great masters that the Gelug tradition eventually became the most pervasively established Buddhist school in Tibet.

12. Most of my submissions regarding the Lam-Rim teachings are taken from the Phabong's teachings that came to me in succession from my teacher G.G. Gyatso who inherited from his teacher Trijang Rinpoche, who in turn received from Phabongkha Rinpoche himself.

8

Stages of Path and other Teachings of Gelug School of Thought

The History of Lam-Rim Teachings

THE GelugPa or the System of Virtue as it can be said is famous for its highly intellectual teachings and commentaries of Buddhist Texts. A practitioner of Gelugpa sect studies maximum of 20 hours a day for 40 years!

The Lam-Rim tradition or the tradition of Graded path has its roots long back in the history of Tibet and India. Actually, it is in the basics of the establishment of the Gelug Pa or Yellow at which is based on the teachings of the great Indian Scholar Atīśa, who is considered to be in the teaching lineage[1] of the famous Indian *tāntric yogī* and saint scholar Nāgārjuna. Although the Lam-Rim teaching is the contribution of Gelug Pa, but more or less all the Tibetan Buddhist give a great respect to these teachings. It is said that the base work upon which this Lam-Rim tradition and Vajrayāna later on established was done by the great Gam Po Pa (1079-1153) who was the chief disciple of Mila Ras Pa.[2] It

1. The Tibetan tradition regarding compilation of a book is that the author must be in the lineage of Buddha. All great teachers are linked with Buddha through the teacher-taught relation. Perhaps this custom was to avoid any heretic views in the Buddhism and to ensure the true teachings of Buddha.

2. *Encyclopaedia.*

was the period when Buddhism of Tibet was historically passing through its inception. Tibet adopted the Lam-Rim tradition for practising its path towards *nirvāṇa* and the Chinese tradition of sudden enlightenment was defeated. Since then a highly consecrated and pious position is attributed to Lam-Rim teachings; by the followers of every sect and sub-sects. This class of teachings is closely associated with Śūnyavāda or the theory of Void along with the theory of cause and effect. Actually, if we analyse the Lam-Rim teachings in the light of Lam Tso Nam Sum, we will find that all the way in his writing, Tsongkhapa has advocated to understand the theory of interdependent relation and the theory of void as interrelated and at some place consider both as one. According to Tsongkhapa, one who sees both of the theory as one, actually understand the dharma. As it is evident from the verse number 11 in Lam Tso Nam Sum:

> After seeing the action and result is infallible and non-quivering and understanding the voidness as both are the same. If you are getting them separately, still you (the practitioner) haven't understood the thought of Śākyamuni.[3]

So, it was the thought of the Indian philosopher Nāgārjuna which was the central idea of Lam-Rim teachings and which was documented by the famous Tibetan reformer and the founder of Gelug sect in Tibet, TsongkhaPa. Nāgārjuna, the chief abbot of Nālandā can be given credit as the first propagator of Śūnyavāda, if not the inventor.

Sudden Enlightenment and Graded Path

To know in some detail of the history of establishment of Lam-Rim teaching, we have to go in the period of Tibetan King (Tib.ཁྲི་སྲོང་ལྡེའུ་བཙན།) Khri Song Dehu Tsen (*circa* AD 740-98) when the introduction of Buddhism was in its primal phase and the Buddhism [which was introduced by Song

3. སྣང་བ་རྟེན་འབྲེལ་བསླུ་བ་མེད་པ་དང་། སྟོང་པ་ཁས་ལེན་བྲལ་བའི་གོ་བ་གཉིས། ཇི་སྲིད་སོ་སོར་སྣང་བ་དེ་སྲིད་དུ། ད་དུང་ཐུབ་པའི་དགོངས་པ་རྟོགས་པ་མེད།།

Sen Gampo (Tib.སྲོང་བཙན་སྒམ་པོ།) has yet to established its firm feet in the land of snow].

The local beliefs of Tibetan people gathered under the leadership of a person named Hashang, who engaged in scholarly debate with the Indian scholar Kamalaśīla who, at that time was in the work of propagation of Buddhism in Tibet. The debate was in fact organized by the king of Tibet himself to show the clarity of Buddhism from Indian and the Hashang view of Buddhism. Actually, Hashang represented the Mahāyāna school of Buddhism in China, which was centrally focused on *dhyāna* or concen-tration. The debate was very fruitful and the Tibetan Buddhist believes that the debate ended with a clear victory of Indian gradualist Buddhism and the defeat of Chinese teaching of sudden enlightenment. So, the debate or council as some calls it, sources agree that the Chinese sudden teaching were popular in Tibet, but they subsequently declined. The widespread disapproval of such doctrine at that time shadow today's practitioners also and among contemporary Tibetan scholars may be seen in the fact that school which speaks of sudden enlightenment often feel compelled to argue that their teachings are significantly different from those of Hāśāng Mahāyāna and is from the Tāntrika school of Vajrayāna. Whether this story is having truth in it or not, it may be questioned, but the presence of this story till date among Tibetan wisdom alone is a proof that in the past somehow there was a conflict between Indian gradual school and Chinese sudden enlightenment and the Indian model eventually won out.[4]

It is said that Hāśāng, with his followers committed suicide after his defeat from Kamalaśīla and Gyānendra. Here I would like to point out one important change in the acceptance of the Buddhist practices in Tibetan Buddhism that is the acceptability to Tibetans. After long passage of time, the emergence of Vajrayāna took place in Tibetan Buddhism and

---

4. Powers.

we know that Vajrayāna advocates for the enlightenment in one lifetime. That means in another way the path of sudden enlightenment.

Furthermore this researcher personally came across with an evidence of the presence of teaching of sudden enlightenment, that I came to know during the direct teaching session from my teacher Lama. That path enables its practitioners to realize *bodhicitta* in one go and skip the seven stages of *bodhicitta* practices as prevalent in Tibetan Buddhism. It is called བདག་གཞན་མཉམ་བརྗེས།[5], which comes as a step in developing *bodhicitta*. What I am trying to emphasize is, that this may be shadow which shows that in the past the Chinese sudden enlightenment, after loosing all its colour, in front of Indian graded school, crept slowly into the rites and customs of Tibetan Buddhism through local folklore. However, it is a mere assessment that in due course of time the teachings of sudden enlightenment crept into the teachings of Tibetan Buddhism that advocated gradual path of enlightenment according to Indian tradition. Now as it can be interpreted that in present time, both the graded path and sudden enlightenment path to *nirvāṇa* are present in the Tibetan Buddhism and are well accepted. They necessarily do not cross each another; rather my teacher told me that both the paths support each other and they deal with different spiritual status of the practitioner.[6] This fact can be derived from the history where we found that a person from བཀའ་བརྒྱུད་པ། sect had started systemizing the teachings of Buddha in the graduated form, which later proved to be the base work for the gradual or Lam-Rim teachings and Vajrayāna.[7] It was already mentioned that this person was GampoPa.

---

5. Literally it means "exchanging your place with others."
6. Geshe Gelek Gyatso, former Teacher Lama at Sera Me college of Sera Monastery near Lhasa, also Reader in Tibetan (Retd.) in the Department of Buddhist Studies, University of Delhi.
7. *Encyclopaedia.*

Having this background of Lam-Rim or the Graded path, we must acknowledge the spirit of Indian scholars in introducing Buddhism in Tibet. The Lam-Rim teaching as it had been and being practised by Tibetan inside or outside Tibet, is broadly divided into three stages as depicted in *Lam gTso rNam gSum,* which is the most inclusive book and enjoys very high status amongst scholars of virtually all sects and sub-sects of Tibet. Most respected book that can be called the Bible of Lam-Rim Tradition is *Lam Rim Chen Mo* (ལམ་རིམ་ཆེན་མོ།) or *The Great Path of Stages to the Enlightenment.*[8] This book can be said to have been inspired from the Atīśa's book *Lamp to the Path of Enlightenment*. This book was translated into Tibet and is called, *Byang Chub Lam Gyi Gron ma* ("བྱང་ཆུབ་ལམ་གྱི་སྒྲོན་མ").

Since *Lam Rim Chen Mo* was a voluminous book. So the author of *Lam Rim Chen Mo,* TsongkhaPa, wrote a small handy book and the essence of entire teachings of Lam-Rim were poured into this work. In another word this small book is an excellent précis work of *Lam Rim Chen Mo*. Undoubtedly this was not an easy job. But the Buddhist scholars have done it and now anyone knowing a little knowledge of Tibetan script can understand the essence of nectar that is present in this small book that is named, *Lam gTso rNam gSum*. In English it means: *Three Principal Paths.* (ལམ་གྱི་གཙོ་བོ་རྣམ་གསུམ།)[9] These three paths are the three *Rim Pas* or the three stages of the path to Buddhahood that is the highest goal of a Mahāyāna practitioner. There are various books on Lam-Rim teachings and they also show us the path towards enlightenment. Several

8. "A particular class of such writings, known as Lam-Rim ("Stages on the Path"), presents the spiritual life as a journey through the varied doctrines and practices of the different forms of Buddhism, arranged on a scale from lowest to highest. Historically, the most influential of these is the lengthy *Lam-Rim Chen-mo* (*Great Account of the Stages on the Path*), written around 1400 by the founder of the Dge-lugs-pa, the dominant order of Tibetan monks." — *Encyclopedia*.

9. Tharchin.

teachers and scholars of Lam-Rim tradition, scholarly contributed their share. Their teachings enriched the Lam-Rim Tradition. They all agree that the Lam-Rim teachings would benefit all human beings.[10]

The Three Principle Stages of the Path

About the three principle stages of the path, all the scholars in the field of Tibetan Buddhism agree that this is the greatest contribution of TsongkhaPa to the Tibetan Buddhism. No other work in Tibetan Buddhism can surpass in the comprehensiveness of the three principle stages of the Path (to enlightenment). The three stages of the path or Lam Tso Nam Sum as they are better known among Tibetan cover the entire essential teaching required. The most amazing thing in this text is the wonderful methodology which TsongkhaPa invented, in order to jot all the terms in extremely concise and perspicuous stanzas, or couplets, mere 14 in number which by any standard is incredible effort.

It is evident from the preceding lines that the three principle path is a triple fold way to achieve the salvation, i.e., *nirvāṇa*. These are:

1. Renunciation or ངེས་འབྱུང་།
2. Bodhicitta or བྱང་ཆུབ་ཀྱི་སེམས།
3. Right View or ཡང་དག་པའི་ལྟ་བ།

Although, these seem to be three, actually they are nothing but understanding the theory of dependent origination as such. In the view of Mādhyamika, all things are devoid of intrinsic nature and this theory comes out from the dependent origination. So to understand the theory of dependent origination is the primal endeavour of any Mādhyamika (to be precise the implication school of Mādhyamikas).

---

10. As usual, we find many Mahāyāna treatises ended with the prayer to almighty that may this benefit everyone. I found this prayer in several books as colophon.

To elaborate, all the three stages are further divided into several steps according to understand the path step by step and with the explained meaning involve in it.

ངེས་འབྱུང་། or renunciation is divided into the following four:

(a) The need of Renunciation
(b) Stopping desire for this life
(c) Stopping desire for future lives
(d) How to know when you found Renunciation.

བྱང་ཆུབ་ཀྱི་སེམས། or bodhichitta is divided into the following three parts:

(a) The need of wish to achieve enlightenment for every living being
(b) How to develop the wish
(c) How to know when you develop the wish.

ཡང་དག་པའི་ལྟ་བ། or right view is divided into the following four:

(a) The need of correct view
(b) What is correct view
(c) How one know the analysis is still incomplete
(d) How one know the analysis is complete.

Suffering

The prime teaching of Buddha is the four noble truths. It is here the teachings and instructions begin at. The way shown by Buddha to get out of the suffering is the eight-fold path, it is here in the right view that the ultimate reality can be understood, the teachings of TsongkhaPa conclude it all for a common man.

We may stop and wonder about that the greatest contribution of TsongkhaPa is limited to the two connotations of the teachings so what is special in it? They are all there in the *Tripiṭaka* or *Kanjur* and *Tanjur*. But the answer is that though the term suffering and right view has been used, but the journey of a practitioner being a GelugPa from the suffering to Right View has very wide meaning and should not be misunderstood as generally used for these terms only. These terms though taken from the traditional texts has been used by TsongkhaPa in their most comprehensive manner for the practice. Although at some stage the similarities can be found, but they are inevitable. After all, both of them are Buddhist teaching for the same purpose, i.e., to achieve enlightenment.

Suffering is the first of the four noble truths. According to Buddhist theory, the state of every being is suffering and the root cause is ignorance or the false knowledge. Suffering as according to traditional teaching[11] is divided into three parts:

1. སྡུག་བསྔལ་གྱི་སྡུག་བསྔལ། suffering caused by suffering itself
2. འགྱུར་བའི་སྡུག་བསྔལ། suffering caused by Change and
3. ཆགས་པའི་སྡུག་བསྔལ། the all Embracing suffering caused by mental formations.

Take a brief note about the above three fold sufferings. The first one is suffering caused by the suffering itself. The explanation is evident etymologically. This type of suffering covers all sufferings which our sense-organs perceive, i.e., pain, sadness. Almost all kinds of people recognize this type of suffering and always search the ways to remove it. For example, even the tiny ant is always busy collecting food to remove the suffering, i.e., hunger.

The second type of suffering is a subtle one. It is suffering caused by change. Most of the people do not recognize it. This type of suffering seems to be happiness but in time changes into a suffering. For example, after coming from outside, we feel hot and the touch of icy cold water feels good. But after some time, it pains us. We are engaged in making money to remove our sufferings, first it gave happiness then it produces suffering: maintaining the wealth, fear of losing it and desire for more.

The third type of suffering is more subtle than the previous one and more difficult to recognize. It is the suffering inherent

11. Rabten.

in *saṁsāra* and is itself the cause of the previous two types of suffering. Our very existence is the root cause of this suffering.

To practice *dharma*, understanding of suffering is the first prerequisite. Without understanding of it, the will to get out of it does not arise. It is like someone being in prison and, not knowing how bad it is, not wanting to escape. If a sick man does not realize that he is ill he does not wish to cure himself. Sufferings are like a wound which does not give pain until it is touched. When a person removes suffering, he attains *nirvāṇa*.

If the first type of suffering is not recognized, one can have no wish to escape from suffering. If the second is not recognized one will try to escape from it in the wrong way and will return to suffering again. If the third type is not recognized, even if one's method is good, one cannot get out to the root of all suffering.

The above three types of suffering has to be understood in the right context according to the teachings of Buddha. It is the suffering that when understood, create the sense of renunciation automatically. It is so because when a person understands the root cause of suffering, he certainly raises his/her status to get out of it and the first step towards salvation is renunciation. TsongkhaPa said in *Lam Tso Nam Sum* that when you've meditated thus and feel not even a moment wish for the good things of cyclic life, and when you begin to think both night and day of achieving freedom, you've found renunciation.[12]

The Cause of Sufferings

The cause of suffering has two divisions:

(A) *Karma* or action, and

(B) Mental Defilements.

---

12. *Lam Tso Nam Sum*, Verse No. 5 says thus:

དེ་ལྟར་བསྒོམས་པས་འཁོར་བའི་ཕུན་ཚོགས་ལ། ཡིད་སྨོན་སྐད་ཅིག་ཙམ་ཡང་མི་སྐྱེ་ཞིང་།
ཉིན་མཚན་ཀུན་ཏུ་ཐར་པ་དོན་ཉེར་བློ། བྱུང་ན་དེ་ཚེ་ངེས་འབྱུང་སྐྱེས་པ་ལགས།།

An unskilful *karma* will lead to sufferings. These unskilful *karmas* are divided into three categories and they are also recognized in the Nyingma school of Buddhism.

1. Unskilful *karma* of body
2. Unskilful *karma* of speech and
3. Unskilful *karma* of mind.

The unskilful *karmas* of body are of three types:

(a) Killing

(b) Stealing

(c) Sexual misconduct

The unskilful *karmas* of speech are of four types:

(a) Lying

(b) Slander

(c) Harsh words

(d) Irresponsible talks

The unskilful *karma* of mind is of three types:

(a) Greed

(b) Wish to harm others

(c) Wrong Views

Mental Defilements (ཉོན་མོངས།)

Mental defilements or *kleśa* is divided into three categories:

(a) Desire [འདོད་ཆགས།]

(b) Aversion [ཞེ་སྡང་།]

(c) Ignorance [གཏི་མུག།]

So the harmful *karma* starts from Desire or Aversion. Desire for wanted or liking things which gave us sensual pleasure and aversion to disliked things. We do *karma* to attach ourselves to desire and detach ourselves from undesired. In both cases the harmful *karma* is accrued which lead to three sufferings.

Now come to the second step of the three principle path, *bodhicitta*.

Bodhicitta

To develop *bodhicitta*, one has to practice the five paths and ten grounds in succession. The five Paths are:

(1) The Path of equipment

(2) The Path of training

(3) The Path of seeing

(4) The Path of intense contemplation and

(5) The Path of freedom.

After the contemplation on the renunciation, the practitioner starts meditating on void. He gets many spiritual powers. He becomes able to know other people's thoughts. Then he acquires the path of equipment and enters into the path of training. After the contemplation that the mind and *Śūnyatā* is one, he enters into the path of seeing and became Ārya *bodhisattva* and, at this stage becomes able to stop his *karma*; no more new *karma* either bad or good. Now from here, the practice of ten ground starts. These ten grounds are:

1. The Joyous
2. The Stainless
3. The Lightmaker
4. The Radiant
5. The very hard to conquer
6. The Turning towards
7. The Far going
8. The Unshakable
9. The Good mind
10. The cloud of *dharma*.

The first ground is reached up to the path of seeing and the other nine are achieved in the next path, i.e., the path of intense contemplation. At each level the *bodhisattva* (the practitioner) gets greater virtue and overcomes greater numbers of defilements. After removing the physical defilements and acquiring the all powers of virtue, the practitioner practices the six paramitas to acquire Buddhahood, which is the highest goal in the Mahāyāna path.

The six *pāramitās*: A *bodhisattva*, who wishes to become a Buddha, has to practice six *pāramitās* or the perfections. They are:

1. The Perfection of giving
2. The Perfection of Morality
3. The Perfection of Forbearance
4. The Perfection of Energy
5. The Perfection of meditation
6. The Perfection of Wisdom.

It is noteworthy here that the five paths and ten ground practices are the same as in the *atiyoga* of Nyingma sect.

The Actual Practice Thought of Bodhicitta

In Tibetan Tradition, the practice to achieve *bodhicitta* is divided into seven stages. These seven stages are considered of very high value and only selected practitioners are to be allowed to do this. The selection is made on the basis of the performance of the practitioner in the past practices. Only the Lama who achieved very high spiritual position can impart this training to their student practitioner. These are as follows:

1. To know all sentient beings as one's mother.[13]

---

13. Commentary on Valid Perception: famed treatise which forms the basis for the study of formal logic in Buddhist monasteries.. It was composed by Master Dharmakīrti in AD 630 in explanation of the *Compendium on Valid Perception* written by master Diññāga in AD 450, great forefather of the Buddhist logic traditions. The reasoning mentioned is found in the second chapter, the "Proof of Infallibility", beginning from line 142 (ff 108b-109a. entry 22).

2. To remember the greatness and kindness of mother.
3. Wish to repay, i.e., sense of gratitude towards the greatness and kindness of mother.
4. Develop the loving and kind attitude towards the beings.
5. Great compassion.
6. Personal responsibility to work for the benefit of others.
7. Feel the juice of the outer achievement of *bodhicitta.*

And the third and final path is correct view. As Tsongkhapa said in *Lam Tso Nam Sum* verse no. 9:

> You may master renunciation and the *bodhicitta,* but unless you have the wisdom perceiving reality, you cannot cut the root of cyclic life. Therefore, make efforts in ways then to perceive interdependence. The sixth of the six *pāramitās* or perfection is wisdom and that enable a practitioner to develop the correct view. As stated above the practice of *bodhicitta* carries very high value in the Tibetan Buddhism. In fact, it is the *bodhicitta* which places the Buddhism above all other religious systems of the globe and the central idea of the *bodhicitta* is great compassion.

The Edge of Prāsaṅgika Mādhyamika

The verse number 14 of the *Lam Tso Nam Sum*[14] says:

> In addition, if you take the view that the things are devoid of intrinsic nature just by seeing and (applying) dependent origination, you'll never be stolen off by the extreme views.[15]

---

14. གཞན་ཡང་སྣང་བས་ཡོད་མཐའ་སེལ་བ་དང་། སྟོང་པ་མེད་མཐའ་སེལ་ཞིང་སྟོང་པ་ཉིད། རྒྱུ་དང་འབྲས་བུར་འཆར་བའི་ཚུལ་ཤེས་ན། མཐར་འཛིན་ལྟ་བས་འཕྲོག་པར་མི་འགྱུར་རོ།།
15. The views of permanence (eternal theory) and annihilations (which negates the existence of everything's); these two theories are considered extreme views in Buddhism and to avoid these two views is in real sense the middle way of Buddha.

The Great Seal

(ཕྱག་རྒྱ་ཆེན་པོ།)

It is a proven fact as I have already mentioned in the earlier chapters that all the sects and sub-sects of the Buddhism in Tibet have inherited in themselves the practice of Tantra. Though it is a quite clear possibility that one sect rely more on the practice part of Tantra and another have inbuilt stress on the practice part of it and the system of the tāntric rites and rituals seem to be different, but in totality the practice of Tantra has a strange uniqueness among the Tibetan Buddhism which is hard to express. As in India the rites and rituals, as well as beliefs are seemingly variable even for a short geographical distance but the overall culture of a bigger area produce a homogeneous society and people of one area happily intermingle with one another within the slight diversity amongst them. This is same in the case of Buddhism in Tibet. A person outside from their society can't assess the difference and sameness of their cultural rites and ritual. But after a little analytical study in detail, the things become quite clear as same in the Phalgu River if one dig even inches, finds water. For example, the Nyingma tradition of Buddhism in Tibet has firm belief in the Terma tradition which incorporates thorough tāntric rites to excavate hidden treasure of Nyingma masters prior to the persecution of Buddhism in Tibet by King Lang Dharma during his short four years rule[16] (AD 838-42). On the other hand, Kargyud school have the masters like Milarepa who, prior to his entrance in Buddhism was a renowned practitioner of black magic and after his initiation in Buddhism included the powers of black magic for the betterment of humankind to keep away the defilements and fight the evil forces. The highlight of the practice of GelugPas as stated earlier in the previous chapter was to raise the intellect of a practitioner to optimum level to be able to understand the true meaning of the Buddha's teachings. In this connection, the Kargyud tradition develops the practice of *mahāmudrā*

16. Shakabpa, p. 53.

which became over-whelmingly accepted in Gelug tradition and after the passage of time became one of the salient features in its tradition. The great seal of the great seal of void as it is described usually, was developed to acquire immaculate virtue and proceed on to the path of enlightenment. The deep root of the great seal is in the *mahāmudrā* practice from Indian system of Tantra and also called the great seal of emptiness which is the essence of the teaching lineage of Atīśa, Nāgārjuna and in Tibet, TsongkhaPa.[17]

It is observed by tḥis scholar that the counterpart of the great seal in the Nyingma tradition is Dzog Pa ChenPo or *atiyoga*. But I can also say after my close observation that both the *mahāmudrā* and Dzogchen should be seen in their own perspectives. The only common thread is the goal, *nirvāṇa*, and compassion which are one of the major pillars on which the Gelug Tradition stands.

Because the non-Buddhist traditions of practices do not realize the self, these get caught in ignorance. In the non-understanding of self, they do not cross all levels of meditation and after crossing the highest point of first *dhyāna* only, fall into egoistic outlook, because the heretical masters maintain a wrong view of self. Vasubandhu once opined that they can't attain salvation through their wrong view of self and they have to go through another method for obtaining salvation.

Buddhist scholars maintain that without abandoning ignorance, which admits (the existence) of a self; there is no salvation. This view of self (*ātmadṛṣṭi*) is of two kinds; that in respect of individual, and that in respect of the elements of Existence.

The *Śrāvakas* and *pratyekabuddhas*, having rejected the theory in respect of *pudgala* (གང་ཟག།, the Buddhist term for soul), have obtained a true salvation in which there is no continuity of rebirth. But the wise *bodhisattva*, if they were to obtain salvation for their own sake only, would proceed as described:

17. *The Blue Annals*.

For there does not exist any one more shameless than he who strives selfishly for salvation, abandoning his family, i.e., living beings whom he did not recognize as being afflicted by birth and death, sunk into the depth of the ocean of phenomenal existence, as if fallen into stream.[18] Therefore, one should search for a method of salvation of living beings. There is none, except Buddha who had perceived the entire method of salvation. Therefore, it is necessary to reject any theory on the substantiality of the elements of phenomenal existence in order to avoid the defilement of knowledge (*jñeyāvaraṇa*). With the help of the theory of Relativity, one will be able to abandon the theory of the substantiality of the elements of phenomenal existence. This last theory will invalidate the first theory because it contradicts the first. Thus one will enter the ocean of scripture (*Āgama*, ལུང་།) and philosophy (རིགས་པ\) in order to establish the theory of Relativity (called ཕྱག་རྒྱ་ཆེན་པོ་ཡེ་ཤེས། or *Mahāmudrājñāna* by Candragomin, which here must be understood in the sense of Knowledge of Relativity or *śūnyatā*, as in the མདོ་ལུགས་ ཕྱག་རྒྱ་ཆེན་པོ་, the *mahāmudrā* according to *sūtra* class), it represents an antidote (གཉེན་པོ) which contradicts that which should be rejected, should be considered as an inference (*anumāna*) obtained by reasoning. The inference must represent a constructive thought (*vikalpa*, རྣམ་པར་རྟོག་པ།). Dharmakīrti maintains that every constructive thought was ignorance (which must be eradicated) but the knowledge of Relativity, which was also stated to represent inference, constructive thought and ignorance cannot be rejected, and because there does not exist an antidote which could contradict an inference, and because all that which contradicts an inference must be false conceptions, and therefore cannot serve as an antidote.

The net conclusion from the above statements by Dharmakīrti, can be inferred as that one should first grasp

---

18. *The Blue Annals* ཉེ་དུ་འཁོར་བའི་རྒྱ་མཚོ་ཁོང་སུ་ཆད་རྒྱུར་པ། ཀླུང་གི་ནང་དུ་ལྷུང་བ་ལྷུབ་སྣང་བཞིན་དུ།
སྐྱེ་ཤི་ཡོངས་པས་ངོམ་ཤེས་པ་དེ་ཡོར་ནས། གལ་ཏེ་གཅིག་ཐར་བྱེད་ན་དེ་ལས་ཁྲེལ་པོར་མེད།།
Candragomin's *Śiṣyalekha Dharmakāvya*, ed. I.P. Minayelf and A. Ivanovsky; vol. IV, p. 77, verse 96.

the notion of Relativity in order to avoid moral defilements. Then in its turn the notion of Relativity should be abandoned, but as it represents an ultimate/true conception it cannot be rejected with the help of reasoning and theories; and thus it can only be abandoned by intuiting the *mahāmudrā* or the Great Seal. Thus this inference, i.e., understanding of Relativity represents the knowledge of *mahāmudrā*. This knowledge can be gained only through the blessing of a teacher or *guru* (through intuition and not reasoning). This is the explanation of "Great Seal" as general doctrine.

Conclusion

SINCE time immemorial the quest of mankind revolves around the secrets of nature. The forces of nature, which regulates the lives on Earth and space, always stimulate the curiosity of human mind. The evolution of Earth and life on it, the life force behind all living beings, these are some of the eternal questions that churn the intellect of every society and religion in every time and space. Perhaps this is the reason why the astronomy and astrology are the subjects that were liked and studied by all the civilization around the globe during all the time.

Even prior to civilized world, the pre-historic and proto-historic man learned a lot about the forces of nature through the regular interaction with them. In its ultimate sense, every religion tries to answer the above-stated questions in order to quench the all-time inquisition of human beings as its regular course. Though very well-known fact that man is mortal and there is no exception to this eternal rule, the efforts were always on to find out the means to repeat oneself on Earth for a longer period, if not forever. To have control over the forces of nature was the first approach of mankind towards his eternal wish to remain permanently on earth. This gave birth to the first link of human being with the deification of nature; the rise of nature-gods. That is why in every faith and belief, the forces of nature are found as the prime gods and, there is always place for description about life after death which attracts the attention of mankind. It can be still visualized in the tribal culture in any part of the world though may be in fractured state. The most popular is the concept of soul which changes the body. Side by side, the non-soul theory which denies the existence of such entity as soul also gained momentum simultaneously and polarize in front of the concept of eternity. These two concepts (soul and non-soul) became the two poles around which innumerable paradoxical theories and philosophy originated. This happens with every concept because wherever one concept has taken a proposition; there come up another proposition opposite to it automatically. For there is East, the West always stands.

Tibet which we know today is either full of myth as Shangri-La of the East, or being neglected by the international community and left free upon the whims of China which claims to having done the peaceful liberation of the Tibet Autonomous region. To respond to its ethnic problem which Tibet is facing the study of its socio-cultural and religious study becomes essential. It's so because it is the historical facts which tell us the root cause of the problems and suggest answers. Tibet nowadays is facing problems on various fronts. It is on the edge of being extinct as an entity; losing its ethnic, social and political uniqueness which it has carried since time immemorial. This is nothing to do with the political independence of Tibet. Actually the path shown by Buddha that Tibet followed has indebt him to share it with the international community. Being one of the staunch followers of Buddhism since AD 700, its cultural and religious roots portray the real individuality of the land and its people. Therefore, to understand Tibet and Tibetan in full length, we have to understand the Buddhism, i.e., the state religion of this country since Song Tsan Gampo till the midst of twentieth century. It is the Buddhist scriptures which tell us about the pre-Buddhist religion and the origin of the civilization in the land of the Snow. The historical, political, cultural, religious and social activity revolves around the religion of this country from the seventh century at the time of the inception of Buddhism till AD 1959. So, by studying the Gelugpa and Nyingma sect, we automatically acquaint ourselves about the lives of Tibetan in full length. According to government (Chinese) sources, the 60-80 per cent of the population of Tibet was Buddhist monks. But according to traditional sources, the 80-90 per cent of the whole of Tibetan people was Buddhist monks and there was uninterrupted tradition of sending the sons of almost all the family to the monastery for study and became novice and then full monks (དགེ་ཚུལ། and དགེ་སློང་།). Only one or two sons left for the household job (ཁྱིམ་བདག །). The monastery was engaged in business, agriculture and even the money-lending job beside its main focus on the study of Buddhist canons. Monks were filthy rich and after the peaceful liberation there was found that Khanpo of the big monasteries used to keep dozen of baskets full of gold. My Lama teacher himself was witness to these times when common man had nothing to eat, the monastery people were counting gold biscuits in their lavish rooms inside the monastery.

Above lines although show the lesser known face of the monasteries, but they cannot undermine the valuable literary and religious contributions of the monastery towards the Buddhism in Tibet. Also, the images built paved the ways of architecture to the new heights. Furthermore, the policy of Buddhism make Tibet more timid and tolerant with its neighbours and we do not found and fierce relation between Tibet and its neighbouring countries from seventh to the mid of twentieth century. Though the introvert nature of lama kings and the geographical situation of Tibet kept it aloof in the international politics beside the 13th dalai tried his best to become a part of international fraternity. These facts required a deep study of the system which Tibet followed so that in the present time, we as the next door neighbour of Tibet whom he considers his *guru*, can judge in the right perspective. This type of research must be done more and more so that we should develop our relation with him in the right context in right direction.

In the west, Tibet serves as a reservoir of unskilled labourers, supplier of the Buddhist iconographic wealth and experts. At the same time in the East, it is unknown, full of myth and superstition besides being road seller of woollen clothes. But the historical relation germane to Buddhism does not support this. Tibet, the land of Lamas, Yaks, mystic *yogīs* and *tāntrics* followed the path that was shown to him by us Indians. Before 1959, it was practising the religious path shown by Lord Buddha and established by the famous Indian Buddhist scholar, Ācārya Padmasambhava and known as Old Sect or Nyingma.

The wheel of time went on around its axis and Tibet experienced many changes in the social, political, and religious life. During the persecution of Buddhism by King Lang Dharma, most of the Nyingma teacher either fled away to cross the reach of king or ceased Buddhist practices. They hid their scriptures in the ponds, in trees, behind rock, etc., which later on became one of the major customs of Terton in Nyingma. The inhabitants of vast area of Himachal Pradesh, almost all of Ladakh region, Sikkim and Arunachal Pradesh are Buddhist by faith and they all follow the Tibetan path. Especially the presence of the followers of GelugPa Path of Buddhism in Ladakh clearly shows the impact of Tibetan Buddhism in that region. In these areas they have Tibetan Lamas in their monasteries. The recent establishment of KarmaPa in the Rumtek Monastery in Sikkim is self-evident. Hence this has an indirect effect in these areas also. Till date, these areas are culturally more nearer to Tibetan than to our mainland. One of the reason behind this proximity can be the presence of climatic as well as geographical similarities, which set them close to Tibet in ancient times. More convincing reason is that they see the Tibetan as resource person and *Kanjur* and *Tanjur* as their resource book and not the mainland Indian Buddhism which practices Hīnayāna, not Mahāyāna. Still in the rocky upper areas of Himachal the magic spell *OṀ MAṆI PADME HUṀ* in Tibetan language can be seen on the rocks. So, this cultural and religious connection since centuries has a definite effect on our relations.

After more than three century of darkness when the religion (ནང་ཆོས) again rose from the forced hibernation the new schools of Buddhism (གསར་མ།) were established because the ruins of old school were still to be collected. Three great traditions of Tibetan Buddhism were established. Among them the highest and strongest was the System of virtues or GelugPa (དགེ་ལུགས་པ།) established by the greatest ever saint produced in Tibet, Losang DrakPa, better known as TsongkhaPa. The other two traditions (Kargyud and Śākya) though continued and there are still some Tibetans who follow them, but the number is too bleak to be recognized. Furthermore, the greater number of Tibetan folk who followed either Nyingma or Gelug assimilated the followers of Śākya by intermingling. The only other tradition is still in vogue is Kargyud which is also the state religion of Bhutan.

The one and only Pre-Buddhist tradition which is still in practice is Bon[1] (Established by Shenrab Mibo). But it has also blushed itself into Buddhism in the way that only the insider can differentiate between a Buddhist practitioner and BonPo. Though it is having distinctive differences both in appearance and practice and the textual catalogue is also dissimilar to some extent from the Buddhistic traditions, but still their outlook is Buddhist.

However, Nyingma practices established by Padmasambhava, still reside and the latest tradition of Gelug has also great followers in commanding positions. To know the differences and similarities between the former and latter is an interesting phenomenon keeping in mind that both claim to be having the practice as true according to Buddhist traditions. That is why I have done this study to benefit the Buddhist scholars and other readers who have interest in the Tibetan community. Although this topic is vast infinitely attracting lots of research work, with this piece of work being the first manifestation of orientation of the insight into the field of Tibetan Buddhism, I have high expectations from the scholar community which according to me should train their intelligence towards this infinitely vast field of knowledge.

1. Bansal.

But more than that, even the systematic study of the Buddhism in Tibet itself creates so much of curiosity and that too, covered with different myths and beliefs that one is forced to infer that Tibetan Buddhism is a secret path in the arena of Buddhism.

This is not true. The Tibetan Buddhism is a way of life and that too, is unbroken system of Mahāyāna since the time of its inception during the period of the great Songsen Gampo. It carries the way of worshipping that was started around thirteen centuries ago by Lord Padmasambhava and refined and defined by the Buddhist Scholars of India and Tibet from time to time as per situation demanded. As I have discussed the rise of Schism within this system in the different chapter entitled "Emergence of Schism in Buddhism," I would only like to mention as a fact which is the result of my research that the different sects and sub-sects in The Tibetan Buddhism are mainly due to two reasons, other factors only depict the impression of time on the religious system which is quite but natural. These two were:

1. The interpretation of the Buddhist Vinaya and other rules in the light of the Buddhism in India, and
2. The indigenous law that intermingled and assimilated from time to time in the Tibetan Buddhism.

Furthermore, the chapter "Emergence of Schism in Buddhism" is in one way an appurtenance outcome of my research work and can be taken as a part of conclusion. However, this area of research needs more attention than a single volume research in order to explore the social, cultural, ethical, and religious relation between the two countries and to explore, debate, experience & research the uncovered areas of the teachings of Buddhism in order to lift it to unprecedented/new/unconquered heights.

Glossary

Bodhicitta: Tib. བྱང་ཆུབ་ཀྱི་སེམས།. The second of three principle paths of stages described by Je TsongkhaPa in his Lam-Rim Chen Mo. The altruistic state of mind in which all sentient beings are considers as same and develops the inner sense of great compassion towards the beings to free an lead them to the path of salvation.

Dalai Lama: The Spiritual and temporal head of Tibet. Dalai lamas are incarnated Lamas and the present Dalai Lama; Tenzin Gyatso, is fourteenth in his lineage from the Gene Drub, the first who was one of the chief disciple of TsongkhaPa, founder of Gelug sect of Buddhism in Tibet. At present Tenzin Gyatso is residing with his government in Exile at Dharamśālā in Himachal Pradesh, India. He is also the recipient of the Nobel peace prize in 1989.

Eightfold path: or Āryaṣṭāṅgikamārga. The path showed by Lord Buddha to get rid form the sufferings and achieve enlightenment. It is classified into three categories of morality, concentration and wisdom.

Enlightenment: Also Bodhi; The realization which Lord Buddha gained under the banyan Tree at Bodh-Gayā on the bank of river Nirañjana. This term is also used as the highest stage of emancipation which a practitioner get and hence the state of mind where the elimination of lust, hatred and ignorance achieved.

Contrary to Mahāyānists, the highest goal of Hīnayānists or Sthaviravādins is *arhat*-hood.

Four Noble Truths: Tib. བདེན་པ་བཞི།. The four Noble truths are: 1. The noble truth of suffering; 2. The noble truth of cause of suffering; 3. The noble truth of the cessation of suffering; and 4. the noble truth of the way to the cessation of suffering.

Ignorance: The root cause according to Buddhism for the all kind of sufferings. The twelve point dependent origination starts here. Buddha preached and Buddhist believes that it is this ignorance which prevents us to see the phenomenal world in its right context. By removing the ignorance, one will be able to achieve the wisdom eye.

Kanjur and Tanjur: The Tibetan classification of the Buddhist treatises. Unlike the Pāli tradition, they included the Tantra as a part of the sayings of Buddha.

Mahāyāna: Budhism split formally into two schools, Mahāyāna and Hīnayāna during the time of King Kaniṣka. The Mahāyāna is liberal one whereas the latter is the group of conservatives who better call themselves as followers of Sthaviravāda, the group of one who follow the actual practice of unbroken lineages from Buddha till day.

Momentariness: The Buddhist term for the theory according to which all things are changing by every moment and are in a constant flux. This very theory is the base of the Buddhist philosophy of no-soul or Anātmavāda.

Renunciation: Tib. ངེས་འབྱུང་། First path or stage of the three principle paths or Stage described in Lam Rim by Je TsongkhaPa. Others two are, *Bodhicitta* and Right view. Etymologically, it is to see the mundane wealth and prosperity as lack of any essence and develop the thought of detachment towards. Finally, to give up the *sāṁsārika* affairs and to become hermit is described as the act of renunciation.

Right View: Tib. ཡང་དག་པའི་ལྟ་བ། one of the eight-fold path as described in Buddhist scriptures. It is the perfect vision of a practitioner and when achieved according to TsongkhaPa, the under-standing that the dependent origination and voidness as one is gained properly. The third and final stage of enlightenment described in Lam-Rim Chen Mo by Je TsongkhaPa.

Shangri-La: The name of an imaginary place found in western literature. Once reached this place, it is stated that the youth stays forever.

Śūnyavāda: One of the four school of thought of Buddhism which advocates the absence of intrinsic nature in all things. Propagated by the famous saint of Nālandā, Nāgārjuna; Almost all schools of Tibetan Buddhism claimed to follow this philosophy. It is also called void.

Terma: During the persecution of Buddhism by the Tibetan King Lang Dharma, the books of Nyingma tradition were hid under the water, in the trees and behind the rocks to protect them from destruction. After the resurgence of Buddhism in eleventh century, the process to unearth the hidden treatises started which is still going on. The process of hiding is called Ter in Tibetan and the procedure to bring out them from their hidden places is called Tenpa. The Tradition of TerTenpa better known as Terma is one of the focal points in the Nyingma practices.

Triple Gems: or the Three Refuges. They are: Refuge in Buddha, Dharma and Saṅgha. One who takes refuge in Triple gems in Buddhist by definition.

Two Truths: Tib.བདེན་པ་གཉིས། . The two truths in Buddhist philosophy are: Transcendental Truth and Universal Truth. Tib.དོན་དམ་བདེན་པ་དང་ཀུན་རྫོབ་བདེན་པ།

Vajrayāna: Claimed to be the indigenous school of Buddhism in Tibet which advocates the Tantra as a system to get salvation within one lifetime.

Bibliography

ཀླུ་གྲུབ་ཀྱིས་བཤེས་པའི་སྤྲིངས་ཡིག། *bShes Pai sPrings Yig "Nāgārjuna's letter"* by Nāgārjuna, Commentary by Venerable Rendawa, Zho-Nu-Lo-Dro, trs. Geshe Lobsang Tharchin and Artemus B. Engle, Library of Tibetan works and Archives, Dharamśālā, HP, India, 1995.

རྒྱན་དྲུག་མཆོག་གཉིས། *Rgyan-drug-mchog-gnyis*, Sikkim Research Institute of Tibetology, Gangtok, Sikkim, 1986.

རྒྱལ་བ་ཚངས་དབྱངས་རྒྱ་མཚོའི་མགུལ་གླུ། *The songs of Sixth Dalai Lama, Tsangyang Gyatso*, K. Dhondup, Library of Tibetan works and Archives, Dharamsala, HP, India, 1996.

འཇམ་དཔལ་ཡེ་ཤེས་སེམས་དཔའི་དོན་དམ་པའི་མཚན་ཡང་དག་པར་བརྗོད་པ། *"Aryamanjusrinamasangiti"*, ed. Durga Das Mukherji, University of Calcutta, Calcutta, 1963

ཐབ་ཟུན་མཛེས་པའི་རྒྱན། Sārnāth edition.

ཡུལ་སྐུ་དོན་གྲུབ་ཀྱི་བོད་སྐད་སློབ་དེབ་དང་པོ། དཔོར་སྤྱན་ཁང་བོད་ཀྱི་ཆེས་མཐོ་རིམ་སློབ་གཉ།, published by Central institute of Higher Tibetan Studies, Sārnāth, Vārāṇasī, UP, 1986

དཔལ་ལྡན་ཨ་ཏི་ཤའི་བྱང་ཆུབ་ལམ་གྱི་སྒྲོན་མ། *Atīśa's lamp for the path to the Enlightenment*, Lobsang Norbu Shastri, Central institute of Higher Tibetan Studies, Sārnāth, Vārāṇasī, 1994.

འཕགས་པ་ཀླུ་སྒྲུབ་ཀྱི་རྩོད་པའི་ཟློག་པ། *The Dialectical Method of Nagarjuna*, Original in Pecha form at Professor G.G. Gyatso, Delhi and in Translated form in English by Motilal Banarsidass, New Delhi.

འཕགས་པ་ལྷའི་བཞི་བརྒྱ་པ། Āryadeva's *Four Hundred Verses*. Personal collection of Professor G.G. Gyatso, Delhi.

རིན་ཆེན་འཕྲེང་བ། *The Precious Garland of Nāgārjuna*, Motilal Banarsidass, Delhi, 1986.

ལམ་གཙོ་རྣམ་གསུམ། *Lam gTso rNam gSum* in Pecha form (manuscripts), by rJe rTsong Kha Pa, personal collection of Lama Professor G.G. Gyatso, Delhi.

ལམ་རིམ་ཆེན་མོ། *Lam Rim Chen Mo "The Great path of Stages"* by rJe rTsong Kha Pa, book published by Tibetan People with help of Palden Yonten Dorje at Majnu ka Tilla (Aruna Nagar) Delhi, AD 2000. Also in the Pecha form at Professor G.G. Gyatso, Delhi.

A History of Indian Logic, S.C. Vidyabhushana, Motilal Banarsidass, 1971.

A History of Modern Tibet 1913-1951, The Demise of the Lamaist State by Goldstein; Melvyn C., Munshiram Manoharlal Publishers Pvt. Ltd. Delhi.

A Lamp for the Path and Commentary, Atisha translated and annotated by S. Richard Sherburne, Jr. Wisdom of Tibet Series-5, George Alken and Unwin Ltd., London, 1983.

A Manual of Key Buddhist Tantra, Lotsawa Kaba Paltsang trs. Thupten K. Rikey and Andrew Ruskin, Library of Tibetan Works and Archives, Dharamśālā, HP, India, 1992.

An Account of Unexcelled Atiyoga of Vajrayana or DzogPa Chenpo Klong Chen Snying Thig: by Rev Karma Wangchuk, Thimpu, Bhutan.

Antiquities of Indian Tibet, A.H. Franke, Calcutta, 1926, chapter II, Nyingma.

Atisha And Tibet, Alka Chattopadhyaya, Calcutta, 20, 1967.

Atisha's lamp to the path of Enlightenment, Geshe Sonam Rinchen and Ruth Sonam, Snow Lion Publication, USA, 1997.

Beyond Eternity through Mysticism, T.D. Bhutia, Doma Dorje Lhaden, Darjeeling, 1994.

Bon: Its Encounter with Buddhism in Tibet, B.L. Bansal, Eastern Book Linkers, Delhi.

Buddha, A Pictorial History of his Life and Legacy, J. Auboyer, Roli Book International, N. Delhi, 1983.

Buddhism in the Tibetan Tradition : A Guide, Geshe Kelsang Gyatso, trs. Tenzin P. PhunrabPa, Routledge and Kegan Paul, London, 1986.

Buddhist Faith and Sudden Enlightenment, Sung Bae Park, State university of New York Press, Albany, USA, 1983.

Buddhist Insight, Essay, Alex Wayman, Motilal Banarsidass, Patna, Bihar, 1984.

Calming the Mind and Discerning the Real, Alex Wayman, Motilal Banarsidass, Delhi.

Chandrakirti's Sevenfold Reasoning Meditation on Emptiness of persons, Joe Wilson, Library of Tibetan Works and Archives, Dharamsala, Himachal Pradesh, 1986.

Commentary on the thirty seven practices of Bodhisattva, Tenzin Gyatso, his Holiness the XIVth Dalai Lama, trs. Acharya Nyima Tsering, eds. Vyvyan Cayley and Mike Gilmore; Library of Tibetan Works and Archives, Dharamśālā, Himachal Pradesh, India, 1995.

Compassion in Tibetan Buddhism, Je TsongkhaPa ed. and trs. Jeffrey Hopkins, Snow Lion publications, Ithaca, New York, USA, 1980.

Drung, Deu and Bon, Namkhai Norbu, Translated from Tibetan into Italian, edited and annotated by Adriano Clemente, Translated from Italian into English by Andrew Lukianowicz, Library of Tibetan Works and Archives, Dharamśālā, India, 1995.

Essence of Buddhism Teachings at Tibet House, 1, New Delhi, 1986.

Ethics of Tibet, Bodhisattva Section of Tsong-Kha-Pa's *Lam Rim Chen Mo*, English trs., Alex Wayman, Sri Satguru Publications, Delhi, 1992.

Four Essential Buddhist Commentaries, His Holiness the XIVth Dalai Lama, Library of Tibetan Works and Archives, Dharamśālā, HP, India, 1993.

Four Essential Buddhist Texts, H.H. The Dalai Lama, First Panchen lama, Jamyang Khyentse Rinpoche, Kalu Rinpoche, Library of Tibetan Works and Archives, Dharamśālā, HP, India 1993.

Heritage of Tibet, W. Zwalf, British Museum Publication Ltd., London, 1981.

Indian Buddhism, A.K. Warder, Motilal Banarsidass, New Delhi, 1970.

Introduction to Buddhist Tantric System, F.D. Lessing and Alex Wayman, trs. from Tibetan Sources, Motilal Banarsidass, Delhi, 1983.

Introduction to Tibetan Buddhism, John Powers, Snow Lion Publication, NY, 1987.

Life and Teachings of TsongkhaPa, ed. Robert A.F. Thurman, Library of Tibetan Works and Archives, Dharamśālā, Himachal Pradesh, India, 1999.

Lo Tsa Ba Rin Chen Bzan Po and Sarma School, Gangnegi, H.P. A PhD Thesis awarded at the University of Degree, 1994.

Mahayana Buddhism: In Particular, NginmaPa Sect, T.D. Bhutia, Delhi.

Nagarjuna's Letter to King Gautamiputra, tr. and ed. V.L. Jamspal, Motilal Banarsidass, N. Delhi, 1983.

Nagarjuna's Letter Commentary by Venerable Rendawa, trs. Geshe Lobsang Tharchin and Artemus B. Engle, Library of Tibetan Works And Archives, Dharamśālā, HP, India, 1995.

Nagarjuniana, Chr. Lindtner, ed. Alex Wayman, Motilal Banarsidass, Delhi, 1987.

Overview of Buddhist Tantra, Panchen Sonam DragPa (1478-1554), trs. Martin J. Board & Losang Norbu Tsonawa, Library of Tibetan Works and Archives, Dharamśālā, HP, India, 1996.

Pali Dhammapada A Reprint of Burma Pitaka Association Publication, 1986, Published by Central Institute of Higher Tibetan Studies; Sārnāth, Vārāṇasī.

Prajna Lexicon/Dictionary Portion of the Sanskrit-Tibetan Thesaurus-cum-Grammar, Sikkim Research Institute of Tibetology, Gangtok: Sikkim, 1992.

Prajnaparamita and Related System, ed. Lewis Lancaster, Berkeley Buddhist Studies Series, 1977.

Religion of Tibet in Practice, ed. Donald S Lopez, Jr. Munshiram Manoharlal Publisher Pvt. Ltd. Delhi, 1998.

Religions of India, ed. Karan Singh, Penguin International, 1985.

Rinchen Zangpo and Renaissance of Buddhism and the Millennium, Giuseppe Tucci, Aditya Prakashan, N. Delhi 1988.

Shisyalekha Dharmakavya of Chadragomin, eds. I.P. Minayelf and A. Ivanovsky; Vol. IV.

Tabo Monastery and Buddhism in the Trans-Himalaya, Thousand years of Existence of the Tabo Chos-khor, O.C. Handa, Indus Publishing Company, New Delhi.

Tales The Thankas Tell: an Introduction to Tibetan Scroll Portraits, Sikkim Research Institute of Tibetology, Gangtok, Sikkim, 1989.

Tantric practice in Nyingma, Khetsun SangPo Rinbochay, trs. and ed. Jeffrey Hopkins, Snow Lion Publications, Ithaca, New York, U.S.A. 1982.

The Blue Annals, George Nicholas Roerich; Motilal Banarsidass, 1976.

The Buddhism of Tibet, Combined Volume, Tenzin Gyatso XIVth Dalai Lama, Nagarjuna and Seventh Dalai Lama; trs. Jeffrey

Hopkins and Lati Rinpoche: Motilal Banarsidass, Delhi, 1975.

The Crystal and the Way of light, Namkhai Norbu, Compiled and edited by John Shane, Routledge & Kegan Paul, New York and London, 1986.

The Dialectic method of Nagarjuna trs. from Sanskrit by Kamleswar Bhattacharya, Motilal Banarsidass, Delhi, 1986.

The Door of Liberation, Geshe Wangyal, Girodias, NY.

The Graduated path to liberation A Rendering in English of teaching given, Geshe Rabten in Dharamśālā in 1969, Publication For Wisdom Culture, New Delhi, 1980.

The Heart of Buddha, Chogyam TrungPa. ed. Judith L. Lief, Shambhala Publication, South Asia Edition, 1999 (Rupa and Co., Delhi)

The History of Buddhism in India and Tibet, Bu Ston, trs. from Tibetan by E. Obermiller, Sri Satguru Publication, Delhi, India, 1998.

The Iconography of Tibetan Lamaism, Antoinette K. Gordon, Munshiram Manoharlal Publishers Pvt. Ltd., New Delhi.

The Identity of Tsu-Chih-Chien, the Tibetan king who died in 804 AD, Erik Haarh, Acta Orientalia, 1963.

The Life of Bu-ton Rinpoche, David S. Ruegg.

The Introduction of Buddhist Tantric Systems, Alex Wayman, Motilal Banarsidass, Delhi.

The Spread of Buddhism and the Buddhist School, N. Dutt, Rajesh Publication, Delhi, 1980.

The symbolization of the Temples of Bsam-Yas, Giuseppe Tucci, East and West, 1956.

The Tibetan Book of Dead, W.Y. Evanswenz, Munshiram Manoharlal Publisher Pvt. Ltd., Delhi, 2000.

Tibetan Religious Art, Antoinette K. Gordon, Munshiram Manoharlal Publishers Pvt. Ltd., New Delhi.

Tibet disappears, Chanakya Sen. Asia Publishing House, Bombay, 1960.

Tibet: Past and Present, Sir Charles Bell, Munshiram Manoharlal Publishers Pvt. Ltd., Delhi, 1990.

Tibetan Tales, Derived from Indian sources, trs. from Kanjur by F. Anton Von Schiefner (in German), trs. in English by WRS Ralston, Sri Satguru Publication, Delhi, 1988.

TsongkhaPa, Three Principal Teachings of Buddhism trs. Geshe Lobsang Tharchin with Michael Roach, Classic India Publications, Delhi, 1990.

Words of my perfect Teacher, Patrul Rinpoche, trs. the Padmakara Translation Group with forwarded by the XIVth Dalai Lama; Vistaar Publications, New Delhi, 2000.

भारतीय दर्शन का इतिहास, प्रदीप कुमार जैन, राहुल पब्लिशिंग हाऊस, दिल्ली 1994.

तिब्बती पाठमाला, टुल्कु दोनडुब, केन्द्रीय उच्च तिब्बती संस्थान, सारनाथ, वाराणसी, बुद्धाब्द 2541 खीस्ताब्द 1917.

भोग देश में माध्यमिक दर्शन, थुबतन छोगडुब, सम्पादक प्रो॰ रामशंकर त्रिपाठी, केन्द्रीय बौद्ध विद्या-संस्थान, लेह, लदाख, बुद्धाब्द 2533, खीस्ताब्द 1989.

संभोट व्याकरण, के॰ अंगरुप लाहुली, केलोंग, लेह।

Journals

The Tibet Journal, Published by the Library of Tibetan Works and Archives, Gangchen Kyishong, Dharamsala, Dist. Kangra, H.P. India.

तिब्बत देश, संपादक विजय क्रान्ति।

धीः, दुर्लभ बौद्ध ग्रन्थों की शोध पत्रिका, संपादक भिक्षु समदोङ रिनपोछे, केन्द्रीय उच्च तिब्बती शोध संस्थान, सारनाथ वाराणसी।

Index